THE O LEVEL BOOK

Martin Stephen is former High Master of St Paul's School, London, and prior to that was High Master of The Manchester Grammar School, only the second man in history to hold both posts. He is the author of numerous academic books on English literature and history, and of the four novels in the acclaimed Henry Gresham series of historical crime thrillers. His latest book is *The Diary of a Stroke*. He is married to Jenny, former headmistress of South Hampstead High School, and has three adult sons.

THE O LEVEL BOOK

GENUINE EXAM QUESTIONS
FROM YESTERYEAR

FOREWORD BY
DR MARTIN STEPHEN
FORMER HIGH MASTER, ST PAUL'S SCHOOL

Michael O'Mara Books Limited

This paperback edition first published in 2016

First published in Great Britain in 2008 by
Michael O'Mara Books Limited
9 Lion Yard
Tremadoc Road
London SW4 7NQ

A CIP catalogue record for this book is available from the British Library.

Papers used by Michael O'Mara Books Limited are natural, recyclable
products made from wood grown in sustainable forests. The
manufacturing processes conform to the environmental regulations of the
country of origin.

AQA (AEB) examination materials are reproduced by permission of the
Assessment and Qualifications Alliance.
Map on pp.54-5 reproduced from 1949 Ordnance Survey map
with kind permission of Ordnance Survey.

ISBN: 978-1-78243-508-2 in paperback print format
ISBN: 978-1-84317-739-5 in Epub format
ISBN: 978-1-84317-740-1 in Mobipocket format

1 2 3 4 5 6 7 8 9 10

Designed and typeset by Martin Bristow

Printed and bound by CPI Group (UK) Ltd, Croydon, CR0 4YY

www.mombooks.com

CONTENTS

FOREWORD

'O' or Ordinary Level exams reveal their age in their name. Nothing in education now could ever be called 'ordinary', any more than a cup of coffee can be called small. Things were simpler back then, an ironic counter to the fact that in some respects O Levels were far harder than any equivalent examination taken today in the UK. The simple element was that those who set O Levels in the early days knew exactly where they were coming from. Only 7 per cent of the pupil body would go to university. To get there, the first hurdle was Eleven-Plus (see *The Eleven-Plus Book*), followed by O Level and then A Level. Back then O Levels were proud to be difficult. No nonsense about enabling pupils here. It was a stinkingly hard, fact-based exam with, from the early 1960s, pass grades of 1–6.

And that's the irony. Difficult it may have been, but actually no one seemed to care much whether you got a grade 1 or a grade 6. The absolutely standard advice given out in schools was that it was the *number* of O Levels one passed that mattered, at whatever grade that might be. I received the only prize I ever won at school for passing all my O Levels. I think I got a grade 1 in Art, a 3 in English Literature and 6s in all the rest. In that fact we could still learn a lot from O Levels. A leading provincial university now only looks at candidates who have a minimum of 8 A* grades in GCSEs, equivalent to eight grade 1s at O Level. No room in the modern world for the late developer, the boy who has spent too much time playing sport or chasing girls, the girl who has spent too much time on her horse or chasing boys. Modern exams are one-strike-and-you're-out, top-grade-only-accepted, actually far more cruel than the ancient O Level. Also, there are unending arguments over whether the standards required to achieve these top grades are, in fact, slipping.

A lot of O Level was about remembering, while the new

GCSE has forsaken memory in favour of asking candidates to think more. Or that's what we're told. Could it be that O Level made one remember *and* think? Maybe that explains why it is still going strong on the international circuit (and making a lot of money for its owners). Something such as the old-fashioned précis of a piece of writing was stultifyingly boring – but what a skill to carry through life if one learnt it. The final story has to be of the old crusty O Level examiner who lost his job to the new wave of exams, but was by oversight left to write the first of the new History exams. He had claimed the ultimate O Level History question was, 'Describe the impact on the life of the average Englishman of Henry VIII's having six wives.' His version for the new-style exam? 'Imagine you are a mole on Anne Boleyn's left buttock and describe your wedding night with Henry VIII.'

O Level may have been dry, but I'm amazed by how much of what I learnt for those exams became buried in my head and acted as the foundation for what followed. Perhaps it's no accident that the O.W.L. exams taken at the best school ever, Hogwarts, are based on O Level. Now, you don't have to be a wizard to answer the questions in this book, but it just might help.

Dr Martin Stephen,
Former High Master of St Paul's School,
May 2008

EDITOR'S NOTES

The O Level (Ordinary Level) was introduced in the 1950s along with the A Level as part of educational reform. It remained the academic yardstick in the UK until replaced by GCSEs in 1988. It is still in use, however, in many former British colonies, and remains a well-respected, internationally recognized qualification across the world. Original O Level pass grades were 1–6, with a 1 being equivalent to an A* at GCSE and a 6 to a low C grade.

In this book you will find genuine questions from 1955–1959 exam papers, including those from compulsory subjects like Mathematics and English Language, as well as optional subjects like Music. Where possible, we have included a few examples of each, so that readers can see the broad range of knowledge and skills required. Papers that would be difficult (perhaps even dangerous!) to try at home, such as the practical papers of Science, Household Cookery and Music, have been left out, so you should find most of the questions 'doable', if tough.

Teaching, and therefore examining, has changed beyond words since the O Level was introduced. Indeed, what might now be recognized as historical or scientific fact, was perhaps unknown or scarcely considered fifty years ago. Formal marking schemes would have varied from year to year, with extensive (and no doubt mind-numbingly dull) instructions issued to examiners for allocation of marks. For example, simply showing your working in Mathematics may have gained you a mark, even if your answer was incorrect. As such, we have included guideline – rather than definitive – answers at the back of the book, written by experts in the individual subjects, so that you can check you are on the right track and compare notes with family and friends. To help you, we have provided a handy section of reference material, including mathematical and scientific formulae and a periodic table.

We hope you enjoy getting competitive with your friends and family members as you tackle *The O Level Book*, whether it brings back fond memories, or stretches your brainpower to dizzy new heights. You will find the time allowance for the original 1950s candidates is clearly indicated at the top of each paper. Finally, here's one question you will soon know the answer to: can you meet the standards of the examinations of yesteryear?

QUESTIONS

ENGLISH LANGUAGE

PAPER I

(One hour and a half allowed)

Answer **three** questions, **Question 1** and **any two** of the
remaining questions.

1. Read the following passage carefully and then answer
   the questions which follow.

The Town Bus

The London Transport Executive's decision to reduce its
bus services by 5 per cent is symptomatic of a malaise
that in time will probably be felt by bus organizations in
most of the big towns. The country bus has a vigorous
(5) present life and a reasonably bright future: it has
already won much traffic from branch railway lines and
seems likely to win more: it can also depend on regular
customers in all villages which are a few miles from the
nearest market town. The town bus, however, has to
(10) meet increasing competition from other forms of
transport, and in many cases the services it offers have
deteriorated. The main advantage of the bus over
suburban or underground railways is in its more
frequent stopping places: it is not so many years since
(15) buses would stop wherever they were hailed, and that,
ideally, is what a bus should do. Congestion in the
streets and bus crews' dislike of too frequent starting
and stopping have combined to push stopping-places
farther and farther apart. The bus, like the train, now
(20) tends to run only between 'stations' and a good electric
train service can win passengers from the bus. In
London this is in fact happening, and traffic on the
underground is increasing as bus traffic declines. High
fares are another major discouragement to bus
(25) passengers; instead of jumping on a bus for a journey
of a quarter of a mile or so people now choose to walk.

The motor-assisted bicycle is often a cheaper means of travelling to work than going by bus, and it offers the additional advantage of independent transport. Buses
(30) are still crowded at peak times with passengers, but these are costly crowds to carry, for to provide enough buses at peak periods means spending money on vehicles and crews which are under-employed for much of the rest of the day. More towns may have to follow
(35) London's example in reducing their bus services, but if this means less congestion in the streets and slightly faster travel for all other road vehicles (including the remaining buses) it need cause no tears. Some reduction in fares is probably the next essential step if town buses
(40) are to avoid running into even greater difficulties.

(With acknowledgement to the *Manchester Guardian*)

(*a*) Summarize the above passage in not more than 120 words. State in brackets at the end the number of words you have used.

(*b*) Give the meaning of *four* of the following words as they are used in the passage:

    (i) symptomatic (line 2)

    (ii) vigorous (line 4)

    (iii) deteriorated (line 12)

    (iv) peak (line 30)

    (v) congestion (line 36)

    (vi) essential (line 39)

(*c*) What exactly is (i) a branch railway line (line 6), (ii) a suburban railway (line 13), (iii) a bus crew (line 17), (iv) a motor-assisted bicycle (line 27)?

(*d*) Explain the placing of the apostrophe in the phrases:

    (i) London Transport Executive's decision (line 1)

    (ii) bus crews' dislike (line 17)

(e) Explain the use of the semi-colon at the start of line 25.

(f) Why are there inverted commas placed round 'stations' in line 20?

2. (a) Give the meaning of the word 'fresh' as used in any *eight* of the following phrases:
    (i) the fresh shoots of a plant
    (ii) fresh eggs
    (iii) fresh meat
    (iv) to feel fresh
    (v) fresh paint
    (vi) a fresh wind
    (vii) fresh air
    (viii) fresh water
    (ix) fresh news
    (x) a fresh complexion

(b) Explain the meaning of any *four* of the following expressions, and give, by means of a sentence, an example of the use of each of these four:
    (i) a gentleman's agreement
    (ii) a Job's comforter
    (iii) a titanic struggle
    (iv) a chip off the old block
    (v) once in a blue moon
    (vi) handsome is as handsome does
    (vii) to carry coals to Newcastle

3. (a) Form the opposite of each of *four* of the following words by the addition of a prefix:

mature, similar, noble, legible, rational, complete

(b) Write down an adjective corresponding to each of *four* of the following words:

voice, credit, spectacle, labour, benefit, example

(c) Compose sentences (four in all) to show the use of *four* of the following:

 (i) *round* as a noun

 (ii) *that* as a pronoun

 (iii) *as* as a conjunction

 (iv) *each* as an adjective

 (v) *off* as an adverb

 (vi) *coin* as a verb

4. (a) Rewrite *two* of the following sentences in order to remove any errors.

 (i) Uncle Tom has agreed to share his money between you and I.

 (ii) The dog had hurt it's paw.

 (iii) The number of accidents on the road are increasing.

 (iv) Crossing the road her heel stuck in a manhole cover.

(b) Choose *three of the following names* and write
(i) a word formed from the name, and
(ii) the meaning of that word.

Olympus; Pasteur; Mars; Titan; Tantalus; Elizabeth.

(e.g. Name: Hercules

Word: Herculean

Meaning: needing great strength to perform, difficult.)

Ref: 260/2 AQA (AEB) Q1, 2 1955; Q3 1956; Q4 1958

ENGLISH LANGUAGE

PAPER II

(One hour and a half allowed)

Answer **three** questions, **Question 1** and **any two** of the remaining questions.

1. Read carefully the following passage and then answer the questions which follow.

The laws governing the guilds were full and complex. Everything, however, worked to a well-laid plan; a plan that, on the one hand, safeguarded the craftsmen themselves from encroachment upon their preserves by
(5) outsiders and foreigners, and, on the other hand, looked after the interests of the general buying public by ensuring that workmanship was always maintained at a high standard, by ruthlessly stamping out any attempts at fraud or deceit, and by the maintenance of
(10) a form of price control whereby any man who either over-charged or under-cut was, to say the least of it, looked upon askance.

While it was the duty of the 'searchers' to travel round the country inspecting the goods made by the craftsmen
(15) and to examine the prices asked, it fell to the wardens to see that suitable punishment was meted out to any who offended against the codes. In short, it was the policy of the guilds to maintain a complete monopoly of their respective trades, rendering it virtually impossible
(20) for any man who was not a member to carry on business with even the slightest hope of success. In return for such a monopoly, however, they automatically provided a guarantee of fine workmanship and honest dealing.

Small wonder, then, that the craftsmen clung to their
(25) guilds as something sacred. Petty squabblings and jealousy there may have been on occasion, yet always was the chaplain behind the scene to serve as the

guildsman's friend, comforter and adviser alike. If the wardens and the searchers demanded, quite rightly, a (30) high standard of workmanship, the chaplains were ever out to bring them together in a common spiritual faith, instilling a healthy outlook on life by arranging regular feasts, by staging plays in which the craftsmen themselves would take the principal roles, and by (35) encouraging all in a spirit of brotherhood, to provide funds for helping the poor and for carrying out structural improvements in their various localities. Indeed, many a town and village today owes much of its charm to the beneficence of those bygone craftsmen, just (40) as some of our noblest institutions trace their origin to various of the City Companies.

In such an atmosphere of goodwill, few craftsmen had any thought but to turn out their best. And even if good workmanship did not come naturally to him, there was (45) always the fear of expulsion to keep him up to scratch! The story of the guilds, with their peculiar lore, customs and beliefs, is as long and glorious as has their influence been great.

Norman Wymer, *English Town Crafts* (Batsford)

(a) Summarize the passage in not more than 140 words, *using your own words as far as possible*. State in brackets at the end the number of words you have used.

(b) Define 'a guild' in one sentence.

(c) In what ways did a guild protect its members? *Answer in your own words.*

(d) Give the meaning of *three* of the words italicized in the following expressions: by *ruthlessly* stamping out (line 8); looked upon *askance* (line 12); in a common *spiritual* faith (line 31); the *beneficence* of those bygone craftsmen (line 39); their peculiar *lore* (line 46).

   (e) Distinguish clearly between *customs* and *beliefs* (lines 46–7).

2. (a) Give briefly the meaning of *four* of the following expressions:

a square deal; a square meal; a square dance; to square a person; to square an account; to square accounts

   (b) Describe, in one or two sentences for each, the kind of work that is done by each of *four* of the following:

an almoner; a psychiatrist; a geologist; a journalist; an accountant; a draughtsman

3. (a) Write down an adjective ending in 'ible' to describe each of *four* of the following:
(e.g. something which can be heard – audible)

    (i) something which can be believed

    (ii) someone not subject to human failing

    (iii) people who are temperamentally unsuited to each other

    (iv) something which can be seen

    (v) something not fit to be eaten

    (vi) something which cannot be read

   (b) Write sentences (*four* in all) to distinguish clearly between the use or the meaning of the words in *two* of the following pairs:

licence	eliminate	inform	official
license	illuminate	conform	officious

4. (a) Rewrite *two* of the following sentences so as to remove any errors or ambiguities:

    (i) As soon as we have lain her new carpet she will give her old one to you and I.

(ii) The reason why the player was dropped was because he disagreed with his captain.

(iii) He ended his letter with 'yours sincerely' instead of 'Yours faithfully'.

(b) Define in one sentence for each, *four* of the following:

a cup; a saucer; a jug; a plate; a spoon; a knife

Ref: 260/2 AQA (AEB) Q4 1956; Q1, 2 1957; Q3 1958

MATHEMATICS

PAPER I

(Two hours allowed)

SECTION A

Answer all the questions in this section.

1. (a) Find the value of $3.14 \, (5.3^2 - 4.7^2)$

   (b) If $\frac{1}{v} - \frac{1}{u} = \frac{1}{f}$, find f when $u = 12.5$ and $v = 7.5$

   (c) An equilateral triangle ABX is described on the side AB of a square ABCD and outside the square. Calculate the angles of the triangle XBD.

2. (a) The area of a trapezium is given by the formula
$$A = \frac{a+b}{2} \cdot h$$
   Express b in terms of A, a and h.

   (b) If $\tan A = \frac{5}{12}$ and A is an acute angle, find cos A and sin $(180° - A)$ without using tables.

3. (a) Solve the equation $\frac{y+2}{3} - \frac{3y-5}{3} + 1 = 0$

   (b) Fig. 1 (not drawn to scale) shows a section of a round bar, 3in. in diameter, on which a flat AB, 2in. wide has been machined.

   Calculate:
   (i) the distance x of the flat from the centre O of the section
   (ii) the angle AOB

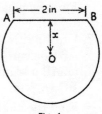

Fig. 1

4. (a) Factorize $6x^2 + 7x - 5$

   (b) Solve the equation $x^2 - x - 0.39 = 0$

   (c) A man's wages were increased from £p a week to £q a week. Express the increase as a percentage of the man's wages before increase.

5. (a) Find the value of $7.3 \frac{(5.2^2 - 2.8^2)}{5.2 - 2.8}$

   (b) A resistance R ohms is given by $\frac{1}{R} = \frac{1}{x} + \frac{1}{y}$

   Calculate x when R = 2.5 and y = 4.5

   (c) An equilateral triangle ABC and a triangle AXC are described on opposite sides of AC. The angle CAX is a right angle and AC = AX. Calculate the angle BXC.

SECTION B

Answer **three** questions only from this section.

6. Construct a triangle ABC in which BC = 3in., the angle ABC = 58° and the angle ACB = 70°.

   Using a ruler and compasses only, construct:

   (i) the circumcircle of the triangle ABC

   (ii) a triangle XBC with BC as base, with area one-half that of the triangle ABC and with the angle BXC = the angle BAC

   Find, by measurement, the length of XB.

7. Draw a line AD of length 10cm and mark off from it AB = 5.8cm. Using ruler and compasses only, describe on AB a triangle ABC in which angle ABC = 60° and BC = 6.7cm.

   Find the angle CAB.

8. A machine which cost £35,000 is operated 8 hours a day in a 5-day week but one hour each day is used for test purposes. For use of the machine there are three scales of charges, the first at the rate of £5 an hour for private use, the second at £15 an hour for research work and the third at £40 an hour for commercial work. It is estimated that the numbers of hours charged at the first, second and third rates are in the ratios 4:2:1. Express the receipts from commercial work as a percentage of the total receipts.

   If the machine cost £30 a week to maintain, how many complete weeks must elapse before one quarter of the original cost of the machine can be recovered?

9. In a triangle ABC, BC = 20cm, CA = 13cm and AB = 11cm.

   Calculate:

   (i) the area of the triangle

   (ii) the length of the perpendicular from A to BC

   (iii) the angles of the triangle

10. (a) Solve the equation $2x^2 + x - 7 = 0$, giving each root correct to two decimal places.

    (b) The volume of a cone varies directly as the square of the base radius and also as the height. Calculate the percentage change in the volume of a cone when its base radius is increased by 10 per cent and its height is decreased by 10 per cent.

Ref: 320/1 AQA (AEB) Q1, 2, 6 1955; Q3 1956; Q7 1957; Q5, 8, 9 1958; Q10 1959

MATHEMATICS

PAPER II

(Two hours allowed)

SECTION A

Answer **all** questions.

1. (*a*) Factorize $3x^2 - 7x - 20$

   (*b*) The temperature C° on the centigrade scale is connected with same temperature F° on the Fahrenheit scale by the relation $C = \frac{5}{9}(F - 32)$. Calculate the temperature on the Fahrenheit scale corresponding to a temperature of 15° centigrade.

   (*c*) Solve the equations $4x - 5y = 22$; $2x + 3y = 0$

2. (*a*) Solve the equation $2x^2 - x - 6 = 0$

   (*b*) In a parallelogram ABCD, the perpendicular from D to AB meets AB in M. If AM = 6cm, MB = 7cm and AD = 10cm, calculate the area of the parallelogram.

3. (*a*) Factorize completely $2ay^2 + ay - 15a$

   (*b*) Solve the equation $3x^2 + 5x - 2 = 0$

   (*c*) The side of a rhombus is 13cm long and the shorter diagonal is 10cm long. Calculate the longer diagonal and the area of the rhombus.

4. (*a*) If v varies directly as t^2 and $v = 180$ when $t = 6$, find the value of v when $t = 1\frac{1}{2}$

   (*b*) If $2l - 1.5d = 12.5$ and $l + 4.5d = 22$, find the value of l

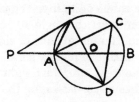

Fig. 2

(c) In Fig. 2, PT is the tangent at T to the circle centre O and AC is parallel to PT. If angle PTA = 32°, calculate the sizes of the angles of the triangle ADC.

5. (a) A class consists of b boys and g girls. The average mark in mathematics for the whole class was m and for the boys alone n. What was the average mark for the girls?

(b) Find the value of t from the formula

$$H = \frac{I^2Rt}{J}$$

when H = 3,500, R = 5, J = 4.2 and I = 3.5

(c) A chord of a circle of radius 15in. subtends an angle of 143° at the centre of the circle. Find the length of the chord and its distance from the centre.

SECTION B

Answer **three** questions only from this section.

6. The cost £y of making a batch of articles depends on x, the number of articles in the batch; y is the sum of two numbers, one of which varies directly as x and the other inversely as x. When the number in the batch is 10, the cost is £28, and when the number is 20, the cost is £44. Express y in terms of x and find the number in the batch when the cost is £37.

7. A vessel in the shape of an inverted cone, with axis vertical and semi-vertical angle 30°, contains water to a depth of 12cm. If a metal cube of side 5cm is lowered into the water until completely submerged, calculate, correct to the nearest mm, the height through which the water surface rises, assuming that no water overflows.

[The volume of a cone = $\frac{1}{3}$ (area of base × height). Take π as 3.142.]

8. (a) Using ruler and compasses only, construct:

    (i) A triangle ABC in which BC = 8cm, angle ABC = 75°, angle ACB = 60°

    (ii) the inscribed circle of the triangle

  (b) Find, by measurement, the radius of the circle (All construction lines must be shown).

9. An aeroplane flying between two airfields takes 16 minutes less on the outward than on the return journey. If the distance between the airfields is 900 miles find the average speed on the outward journey if it exceeds that on the return journey by 20mph.

10. Fig. 3 shows a key-way cut from a circular plate. Calculate the length of AB.

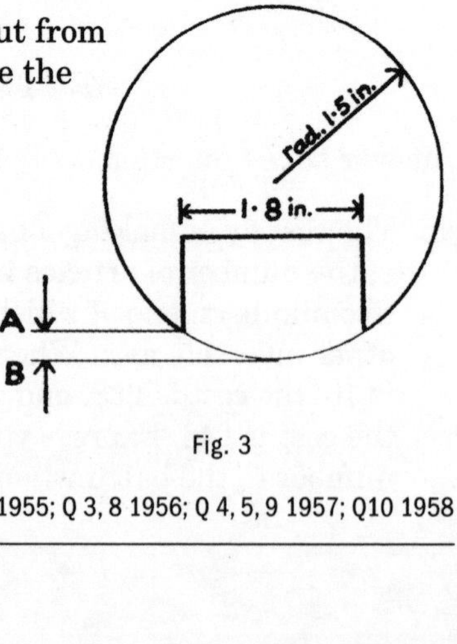

Fig. 3

Ref: 320/2 AQA (AEB) Q1, 2, 6, 7 1955; Q 3, 8 1956; Q 4, 5, 9 1957; Q10 1958

MATHEMATICS

PAPER III – GENERAL

(Two and a half hours allowed)

Answer **six** questions only.

All questions carry equal marks.

1. (a) Solve the simultaneous equations:
$$4x - y = 4$$
$$4x^2 + xy = 6y$$

   (b) The life of a carbide steel-cutting tool is given by the formula
$$T = \left(\frac{708}{v}\right)^{5.2}$$

   Find T if $v = 450$.

2. Two points A and B are in the same horizontal plane as C, the foot of a tower CD. The angle $ABC = 76°$ and $AC = BC = 60$ft. The elevation of D, the top of the tower, from A is $54°$. Calculate the height of the tower and the elevation of D from the mid-point of AB.

3. (a) The time of oscillation of a pendulum is given by the formula
$$T = 2\pi\sqrt{\left(\frac{1}{32.2}\right)}$$

   Calculate l when $T = 1.45$

   (Take π as 3.14)

   (b) If $i = 15 \sin(100\pi t)$, find i when $t = 0.005$

4. Sketch the curve $y = x(4-x)$ for values of x from 0 to 4. Find:

   (i) the area enclosed by the curve and the x-axis

   (ii) the volume obtained by rotating the area about the x-axis

5. The relation between the volume V of steam and its pressure P is given by the formula

$$PV^{17/16} = 475$$

Calculate

    (i) P when V = 4.26

    (ii) V when P = 125

6. (*a*) Solve the equation $3x^2 - x - 6 = 0$, giving each root correct to two decimal places.

   (*b*) Solve the equations

$$2x - y = 3 \qquad x^2 + 2y^2 = 6$$

7. The formula $d = \sqrt[3]{\dfrac{320RC^2}{t}}$ relates to overhead cables.

Calculate d when $R = 1.7 \times 10^{-6}$, $t = 21$ and $C = 265$

8. In a triangle ABC, BC = 7cm, CA = 6cm and AB = 8cm. The bisector of the angle A meets BC at X and the bisector of the angle B meets CA at Y. Calculate the angle C and the length of XY.

9. Each edge of a regular tetrahedron is of length l.

Show that the volume of the tetrahedron is $\dfrac{l^3\sqrt{2}}{12}$

Calculate, correct to the nearest mm, the radius of a sphere equal in volume to a tetrahedron of edge 13cm. (Take π as 3.142.)

10. In Fig. 4, RAQ is a tangent at A to the circle ABC. The lines BQ and CR are perpendicular to the tangent and AP is perpendicular to BC.

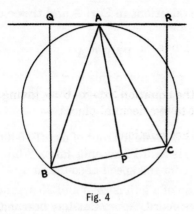

Fig. 4

Show that: $\dfrac{BQ}{AP} = \dfrac{AP}{CR}$

Ref: 320/3 AQA (AEB) Q1, 2 1955; Q3 1956; Q4, 5 1957; Q6, 7, 8, 9 1958; Q10 1959

GENERAL SCIENCE
PAPER 1A
(Two hours allowed)

Answer **all** the questions in Part A and **three** questions from Part B.

PART A

Answer **all** the questions in this part.
You are advised to spend not more than three-quarters of an hour on this part.

1. (*a*) A sound is made in front of a cliff 1000ft away. An echo is heard 2 seconds later. What value does this give for the speed of sound in air?

   (*b*) The flash of a gun is seen and 25 seconds later the sound is heard. Approximately how many miles away is the gun?

2. Both steel and soft iron are magnetic substances. Which would you use:

   (*a*) in making a permanent magnet?
   Reason:

   (*b*) in making an electro-magnet?
   Reason:

3. (*a*) Is air a mixture or a compound?

   (*b*) What are the four main constituents of atmospheric air?

   (*c*) In what proportions are the two chief constituents present?

4. Complete the following equations:

   (*a*) Sodium + water → ....+..............

   (*b*) Limestone (on heating) → ....+..............

   (*c*) $CaO + H_2O$ → ....

5. A plant is illuminated from one side only. What will be the effect on the following:

(*a*) shoot (or stem)?

(*b*) leaves?

(*c*) roots?

6. This is a diagram of a human tooth.

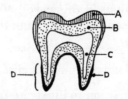

Name A, B, C and D.

7. (*a*) Complete:

Light travels in _____ lines as long as it is travelling in _____ medium. The bending of a ray of light as it passes from air to water is called _____.

(*b*) What effect does this have on the apparent depth of a pond?

8. Complete the following table:

Common Name	Chemical Name	Formula
Common salt		
Washing soda		
Quicklime		

9. (*a*) All acids:

(i) Contain the element _____

(ii) React with _____ substances to form salts and water

(iii) Turn _____ litmus _____

(*b*) Name three acids.

10. Briefly describe what is **observed** to happen when:

    (a) A piece of sodium is placed on water

    (b) Carbon dioxide is passed into lime-water for a short time

    (c) Carbon dioxide is passed into lime-water for a long time

11. Name two functions of (a) the leaf and (b) the root of a green plant.

    (a) The leaf   (i) _____   (ii) _____

    (b) The root   (i) _____   (ii) _____

12. Write a word equation to illustrate the process of photosynthesis.

13. Write down three characteristic features of mammals.

14. State three reasons why you consider mercury to be a good liquid for use in a thermometer:

    (i) _____

    (ii) _____

    (iii) _____

15. Calculate the resulting maximum temperature of the mixture when 25g of water at 100°C are added to 50g water at 10°C, and the mixture well stirred.

PART B

Answer **three** questions only from this part.

16. (a) By means of a labelled diagram show the structure of the human eye.

    (b) What condition causes short sight and how can this be corrected?

17. (a) Explain why more soap is required for washing in hard water than in rainwater.

(b) (i) What is an emulsion? (ii) Name the substance responsible for the emulsification of fats in the human body (iii) Where is it produced and where are the fats emulsified?

18. (a) What are the main constituents of urine?

(b) Describe briefly how urine is formed.

(c) How would you test a sample of urine for
(i) acidity (ii) the presence of chlorides?

19. Explain the following statements:

(a) A dentist uses a concave mirror to examine a patient's mouth. He usually warms it before using it for this purpose.

(b) A flower which is purple in daylight appears to be red when seen in the light of an electric lamp.

(c) A potted plant is kept in a room which has only one window. The plant is placed near the window but, to avoid lopsided growth, it is rotated at regular intervals during the daytime so that at first one side of the plant and then the other faces the window.

20. Give an account of the role of bacteria in **three** of the following:

(a) a decaying tooth

(b) the souring of milk

(c) fixation of atmospheric nitrogen in leguminous plants

(d) a compost heap

Ref: 3878/1 AQA (AEB) Q1–6, 16 1955; Q7–13 1956; Q14, 15, 17, 18 1957; Q19, 20 1958

GENERAL SCIENCE

PAPER 1 B

(Two hours allowed)

Answer **all** the questions in Part A and **three** questions from Part B.

PART A

Answer **all** the questions in this part.

You are advised to spend not more than three-quarters of an hour on this part.

1. State the colour of each of the following substances:
   (a) Mercuric oxide
   (b) Anhydrous copper sulphate
   (c) Potassium chlorate
   (d) Sulphur dioxide

2. (a) What substances are formed by the action of hydrogen on heated copper oxide?
   (b) What name is given to this type of chemical action?
   (c) Give one other example of the same type of action.

3. Insert after each of the following the letter E, M or C to indicate whether it is an element, mixture or compound:

   Iron ( ); Common salt ( ); Brine ( ); Water ( );
   Hydrogen ( ); Washing soda ( ); Air ( )

4. (a) Write a word equation to illustrate the process of fermentation by yeast.
   (b) State two purposes for which yeast is used by man:
      (i) _____ (ii) _____

5. (a) Name the digestive juice containing pepsin.

   (b) State the reaction promoted by pepsin.

6. (a) What causes the souring of milk?

   (b) Explain briefly why (i) oats may be preserved by drying; (ii) beef may be preserved by refrigeration.

7. Place the number of the word in Column B in its appropriate place in Column A:

Column A	Column B
____ Transference of heat by moving liquids	1. Conduction
____ A liquid which is a good conductor of heat	2. Convection
	3. Winds
____ Transference of heat by molecules striking against molecules	4. Mercury
	5. Radiation
	6. Water
____ Convection currents in the atmosphere	7. Thermos flask
____ Heat travels by rays in this process	
____ This keeps hot liquids hot and cold liquids cold	

8. Complete the following statements:

   (a) The ____ energy of water at the top of a waterfall is converted to ____ energy as it falls.

   (b) The energy in an accumulator is converted to ____ energy and ____ energy in the headlamp of a car.

   (c) In what part of the arm is energy liberated?

   (d) What is the source of this energy?

9. Complete the following statements

   (a) The lightest known element is _____.

   (b) When a direct electric current is passed through dilute sulphuric acid, _____ is liberated at the cathode and _____ at the _____. The ratio by volume of the first gas to the second gas is _____ to _____. The electrodes are made of _____.

10. (a) Name four different types of teeth found in the human mouth.

    (b) What is the main substance of which a tooth is made?

11. (a) Define the term *element*.

    (b) Name the four essential elements present in protein.

12. Give the name of:

    (a) the pores present in the epidermis of the green leaf

    (b) the green pigment in the cells of leaves

    (c) What gaseous exchange takes place through the pores of the leaf during:

        (i) daylight

        (ii) night-time?

13. State what is measured by the following instruments:

    (a) a barometer

    (b) a hygrometer

    (c) a thermometer

14. (a) State what is measured in the following units:

        (i) volts

        (ii) ohms

        (iii) amperes

    (b) Give the relationship that exists between these three units.

15. Give the chemical names of:
   (a) the liquid in a lead plate accumulator
   (b) the liquid in a Leclanché cell
   (c) a gas which can be burnt with oxygen to give a flame used for welding
   (d) an important constituent of coal gas

PART B

Answer **three** questions only from this part.

16. (a) State the two laws of reflection of light.
   (b) Describe how you would verify *one* of them.

17. (a) Why is iron classed as a metal and nitrogen as a non-metal?
   (b) In what forms do plants and animals obtain their nitrogen?

18. (a) Define *latent heat of melting of ice* and describe a simple experiment to find its value. (b) Why does a layer of snow take a considerable time to melt on a sunny day? Explain how snow protects vegetation when days are warm and nights are cold.

19. (a) Explain the construction and working of an electric bell.
   (b) Why would an armature on the clapper made of (i) steel, (ii) plastic material be unsuitable?

20. Describe:
   (a) an experiment to show that water is a compound of oxygen and hydrogen
   (b) a laboratory method of preparing pure water from tap water

Ref: 387/1 AQA (AEB) Q18 1955; Q17, 19, 20 1956; Q1-6 1957; Q7-12 1958; Q18 1959

GENERAL SCIENCE

PAPER IIA

(Two hours allowed)

Answer **all** the questions in Part A and **three** questions from Part B.

PART A

Answer **all** the questions in this part. Write your answers in the space provided.

You are advised to spend not more than three-quarters of an hour on this part.

1. The diagram illustrates an eclipse.

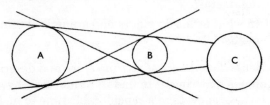

   (*a*) If it is an eclipse of the sun then:

      A is the _____

      B is the _____

      C is the _____

   (*b*) If it is an eclipse of the moon then:

      A is the _____

      B is the _____

      C is the _____

2. (*a*) Why does red cloth appear red in ordinary sunlight?

   (*b*) What colour would red cloth appear if the light falling on it were blue?

   (*c*) Why are white clothes worn in hot climates?

3. Given iron and steel and aluminium, which would you use:

   (*a*) Where rusting must not occur?

   (*b*) Where lightness in weight is the chief consideration?

   (*c*) Where hardness is the chief consideration?

4. (*a*) What two substances are essential for photosynthesis?

   (*b*) Give two conditions which are necessary for photosynthesis

   (*c*) Name two end products

5. What is meant by a reflex action?

6. Complete:

   The largest planet is named_____.

   The planet furthest from the sun is named_____.

   The planets_____and_____ both travel once round their orbits in fewer than 365 days.

7. In what units would you measure the following:

   (*a*) An electric current?

   (*b*) The resistance of a conductor?

   (*c*) The E.M.F. of a cell?

8. Complete the following equations:

   (*a*) sodium hydroxide + hydrochloric acid =

   (*b*) calcium carbonate + dilute hydrochloric acid =

   (*c*) sodium bicarbonate (on heating) =

9. (*a*) Is oxygen more, or less, soluble in hot water than cold?

(b) State which of the following are soluble and which are insoluble in water:

  (i) sodium chloride

 (ii) sodium carbonate

(iii) calcium carbonate

(iv) calcium bicarbonate

 (v) calcium hydroxide

(vi) carbon dioxide

(vii) iron

(viii) sand

10. When coal is heated in the absence of air, four chief products are formed. Name them.

11. (a) In the drawing of the germinating broad bean seed, name 1–5.

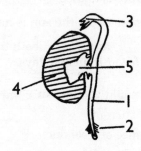

(b) Give two conditions required for the germination of seeds.

12. (a) What pigment in the human blood absorbs oxygen?

(b) In what part of the blood is this pigment carried?

(c) What chemical changes occur to the pigment in (i) the lungs; (ii) the muscles.

13. (*a*) What is *humus*?

(*b*) Why is humus a beneficial constituent of the soil for plants?

(*c*) Why is a waterlogged soil detrimental to the growth of most plants?

14. (*a*) State the *Principle of Archimedes*.

(*b*) Why would it be easier for you to float in sea water than in fresh water?

(*c*) A metal cube weighs 20g in air and 16g in water

   (i) What is its volume?

   (ii) What is its density?

15. Complete the following statements.

(*a*) Sound waves will not travel through _____.

(*b*) The velocity of sound in air is approximately

   _____.

(*c*) The sound waves entering the outer ear cause the _____ to vibrate. The vibration of this is carried across the middle ear by _____. In the inner ear is the real organ of sound which is called the _____.

PART B

Answer **three** questions only from this part.

16. (*a*) Explain what is meant by convection of heat, and describe an experiment to illustrate it in the case of a liquid.

(*b*) Why does a closed room containing a number of people get 'stuffy'? Explain how a coal fire assists in the ventilation of a room.

17. (*a*) Explain why water from chalk and limestone regions is 'hard', while that from granite regions is 'soft'.

(*b*) Distinguish between 'temporary hardness' and 'permanent hardness' of water. Give one method by which 'total hardness' may be removed.

18. (*a*) What percentages by volume of nitrogen, oxygen and carbon dioxide occur in the atmosphere?

(*b*) Describe how green plants, animals and saprophytes help to maintain constant proportions of oxygen and carbon dioxide in the atmosphere.

19. (*a*) Describe concisely the function of the heart.

(*b*) At what part of the circulatory system would you expect the pressure to be highest?

20. (*a*) What can be *seen* to happen when an electric current is passed through:

   (i) a very thin wire

   (ii) a solution of copper sulphate (using platinum electrodes)

   (iii) a horizontal coil of wire with a compass needle placed above one end and free to swing in a vertical plane?

(*b*) State what difference (if any) would be observed if the current were reversed in each case.

Ref: 387/2 AQA (AEB) Q1–5, 16 1955; Q6–12, 17, 18 1956; Q13, 19 1957; Q14, 15, 20 1958.

GENERAL SCIENCE

PAPER IIB

(Two hours allowed)

Answer **all** the questions in Part A and **three** questions from Part B.

PART A

Answer **all** the questions in this part. Write your answers in the space provided.

You are advised to spend not more than three-quarters of an hour on this part.

1. Water in a trough is 10cm deep.
   (*a*) What is the pressure of the water at the bottom of the trough?
   (*b*) If the area of the bottom of the trough is 80sq.cm, what force is exerted on it by the water?

2. (*a*) State Ohm's Law.
   (*b*) What current could be produced by a 6-volt battery in a circuit of total resistance 5 ohms?

3. (*a*) State the two chief substances which cause the rusting of iron.
   (*b*) State two methods by which the rusting of iron may be prevented.

4. From the following list underline three substances which dissolve in dilute sulphuric acid.

   copper   chalk   zinc   iron
   copper sulphate   zinc oxide

5. (a) Name and state the law which gives the relation between the extension of a spring and the weight suspended from it.

   (b) A tub of coal is weighed first at the bottom of the pit and then at the top of the shaft. A spring weighing machine is used on both occasions.

   Would there be any difference between the weights recorded?

   Give reasons for your answer.

6. (a) Say whether each of the following chemicals is an acid, an alkali or a salt:

     (i) Ammonium hydroxide

     (ii) Ammonium sulphate

   (b) Why is ammonium sulphate important as an agricultural fertilizer?

7. (a) Define the term *diffusion*.

   (b) Give an example of this process as it occurs in

     (i) an animal

     (ii) a plant

8. From the following list – anode, tungsten, armature, voltmeter, voltameter, manganese dioxide, commutator, transformer, ohm – choose:

   (a) The name of a scientist

   (b) A metal used in electric light filaments

   (c) The moving part of a motor

   (d) A depolarizing agent

   (e) Current reverser in a motor

   (f) Cell used in electrolysis experiments

9. (*a*) Name the element (or elements) present in:
   (i) graphite
   (ii) sulphuric acid
   (iii) sugar

(*b*) By writing C for compound, M for mixture, indicate the nature of the following substances:
   (i) coal tar
   (ii) chalk
   (iii) milk

10. (*a*) Name the type of thermometer used to take the temperature of the human body.

(*b*) What liquid is contained in this thermometer?

(*c*) What is the purpose of the constriction in it?

(*d*) How is the thermometer reset for further use?

(*e*) Why is it not sterilized with boiling water?

(*f*) What is the normal temperature of the healthy human body?

11. Fill in the blank spaces where indicated.

The _____ of the root of a plant absorb water from the soil by the process of _____.

Water vapour is given off through the _____ of the leaves of a plant and this process is called _____.

When water is given off from the leaves more quickly than it is absorbed from the soil, the plant _____.

12. (*a*) Name the final products of digestion in the human body of:
   (i) starch
   (ii) proteins
   (iii) fats

(b) In what part of the alimentary canal does starch digestion occur?

13. (a) How would you test a given foodstuff for protein?

(b) Name three foods rich in protein.

14. (a) Name two conditions favourable to the growth of bacteria.

(b) Give four ways in which food may be preserved from bacterial action.

15. (a) Where would an object have to be placed to give an erect image in a concave mirror?

(b) Name a common use of this arrangement.

(c) What is the difference between a real and a virtual image?

PART B

Answer **three** questions only from this part.

16. Explain:

(a) Why the spout of a teapot reaches at least as high as the lid

(b) Why there is a risk of cracking a thick glass tumbler if very hot water is poured into it quickly

(c) How birds conserve their heat in winter

(d) How a fire in an open grate helps to ventilate a room

17. Give an account of the interdependence of green plants, animals and saprophytes.

18. Explain why:

(a) the action of frost is beneficial to the soil

(b) grass seed will usually germinate more rapidly in August than in March in Great Britain

(c) sweating causes a cooling of the body

(d) at high altitudes it is necessary to inhale oxygen from cylinders

19. (a) Describe how quicklime is obtained on a large scale.

(b) Describe and explain what is observed when quicklime is treated with (i) a little water; (ii) excess water.

(c) Explain the effect of lime on the soil and name *two* other uses of lime.

20. Describe the construction and method of working of the internal combustion engine.

Ref: 387/2 AQA (AEB) Q13, 14 1955; Q15 1956; Q1-4, 16 1957; Q5-7, 18 1958;
Q8-12, 17, 19, 20 1959

HISTORY

First Syllabus – An outline of the History of Great Britain

(Two and a half hours allowed)

Answer **five** questions from any **two** of the following sections.

Not more than **three** questions are to be answered from any one section.

SECTION A 1066–1485

SECTION B 1485–1603

SECTION C 1603–1760

SECTION D 1760–1870

SECTION E 1870–1939

Credit will be given for sketch-maps and diagrams where they are appropriate.

SECTION A 1066–1485

1. What action did William I take after the Battle of Hastings to strengthen the Norman power in England?

2. What were the main events leading up to King John's acceptance of the Magna Carta? What do you consider to be its most important provisions?

3. Indicate the causes, and describe the course and results, of the Peasants' Revolt, 1381.

4. Describe the part played in the disputes between the Lancastrians and the Yorkists by Warwick the King Maker.

5. What reforms were introduced in England by Henry II?

6. Why is John usually considered to have been a bad King?

7. Describe the open field system of arable farming.

8. Why is Edward I considered a great King?

SECTION B 1485–1603

9. What action did Henry VII take to strengthen his power after his accession?

10. Trace the course of the Reformation in England under Henry VIII.

11. Describe the causes and the course of Anglo-Spanish rivalry under Elizabeth I.

12. What religious difficulties did Elizabeth I face on her accession, and how did she deal with them?

13. What religious changes were introduced during the reign of Edward VI?

14. Why was the Elizabethan Poor Law of 1601 necessary? Describe its provisions.

15. Why was there economic distress in England in Tudor times and how did Tudor governments deal with this problem?

16. Show how English sea power was developed during the Tudor period.

SECTION C 1603–1760

17. What events led up to the flight of James II from England in 1688?

18. Why did England enter the War of the Spanish Succession? What did she gain from the Treaty of Utrecht, 1713?

19. Describe the main causes of dispute between James I and his Parliaments.

20. Describe the religious changes that followed the Restoration.

21. What did Sir Robert Walpole achieve for England?

22. Why did the Whigs control the government of Great Britain during the period 1715–1760?

23. Why was there a revolution in 1688?

24. Outline the growth of British colonization in North America between 1640 and 1715.

SECTION D 1760–1870

25. What grievances led the American colonists to issue the Declaration of Independence in 1776?

26. Explain why there was serious discontent in Great Britain between 1815 and 1822.

27. What was Great Britain's contribution to the defeat of Napoleon?

28. Describe the measures taken by George III to undermine the power of the Whigs.

29. Compare village life in England in the middle of the nineteenth century with village life at the accession of George III.

30. Trace the steps by which England adopted the policy of 'Free Trade' in the nineteenth century.

31. Why did Britain lose the war against the American colonists?

32. Write an account of the changes in transport that took place during the reign of George III, 1760–1820.

SECTION E 1870–1939

33. What steps were taken by the Conservative government of Disraeli (1874–1880) to improve social conditions in Great Britain?

34. Why did Britain go to war in 1914?

35. What were the main developments in trade unionism in England, (a) between 1871 and 1914, and (b) between 1914 and 1927?

36. What was done by the Liberal governments between 1906 and 1914 to improve the conditions of the people?

37. Outline the main stages in the career of J. Ramsay Macdonald.

38. What were the main causes of social unrest in Britain after the First World War?

39. Why was British agriculture depressed after 1873? What steps were taken to deal with the problem before 1914?

40. Why did Britain go to war in 1939?

Ref: 300/1 AQA (AEB) Q2, 3, 9, 10, 11, 12, 17, 18, 25, 26, 33, 34 1955; Q1, 5, 13, 19, 20, 21, 27, 35 1956; Q6, 7, 14, 28, 29, 36, 37, 1957; Q4, 8, 15, 16, 22, 30, 39, 40 1958; Q23, 24, 31, 32, 38 1959.

HISTORY

Second Syllabus – Britain and World Affairs from 1870

(Two and a half hours allowed)

Answer **five** questions. Not more than **three** questions are to be answered from any one section. At least one question must be answered from Section A and one from Section B. Credit will be given for sketch-maps and diagrams where they are appropriate.

SECTION A 1870–1914

1. What were the causes of the expansion of the British Empire during the period 1870–1914?

2. Explain how and why British industrial supremacy was challenged during the closing years of the nineteenth century.

3. Trace the steps by which Great Britain after 1900 abandoned her policy of 'splendid isolation' from Continental affairs.

4. (a) Define the meaning of the term 'inter-imperial preference'.

   (b) Describe and account for the growth of inter-imperial preference in the British Empire after 1897.

5. What were the main features of British foreign policy between 1900 and 1914?

6. Explain the importance of the opening of the Suez Canal in 1869 in promoting the growth and development of the British Empire.

SECTION B 1914–1939

7. What difficulties did Britain face in India between the two World Wars?

8. Why did Great Britain declare war on Germany in 1939?

9. What were the main European problems that the Peace Conference of 1919 had to deal with?

10. Describe the Covenant of the League of Nations.

11. In 1933 Congress gave Franklin D. Roosevelt more power than any American President had ever before exercised in time of peace. What were these powers and why were they given to the President?

12. Describe in outline the British campaigns against the Ottoman Empire during the First World War.

SECTION C AFTER 1939

13. What were the main achievements in foreign affairs of the Labour government of Mr Attlee (1945–1950)?

14. What issues have caused friction between the Western Powers and the USSR since the defeat of Hitler?

15. Discuss the difficulties facing the Lancashire cotton trade.

16. Compare the attitude of the United States to European affairs after the Second World War with its attitude after the First World War.

17. What problems had Winston Churchill to deal with when he became Prime Minister in May 1940?

18. Describe the problems facing the rulers of India and Pakistan when the British Empire in India came to an end on August 10th, 1947.

Ref: 301/1 AQA (AEB) Q1, 2, 3, 7, 13, 14 1955; Q4, 5, 8, 15 1956; Q6, 9, 16, 1957; Q10, 11, 17, 18 1958; Q12 1959

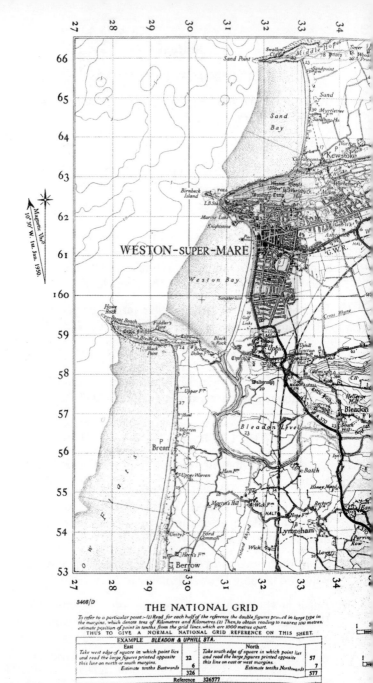

3408/D

THE NATIONAL GRID

To refer to a particular point:—(1) Read, for each half of the reference the double figures printed in large type in the margins, which denote tens of Kilometres and Kilometres. (2) Then, to obtain reading to nearest 100 metres, estimate position of point in tenths from the grid lines, which are 1000 metres apart.

THUS TO GIVE A NORMAL NATIONAL GRID REFERENCE ON THIS SHEET.

EXAMPLE	BLEADON & UPHILL STA.		
East		**North**	
Take west edge of square in which point lies and read the large figures printed opposite this line on north or south margins.	32	Take south edge of square in which point lies and read the large figures printed opposite this line on east or west margins.	57
Estimate tenths Eastwards	6	Estimate tenths Northwards	7
	326		577
Reference	326577		

MAP FOR GEOGRAPHY QUESTION 1 (OVERLEAF)

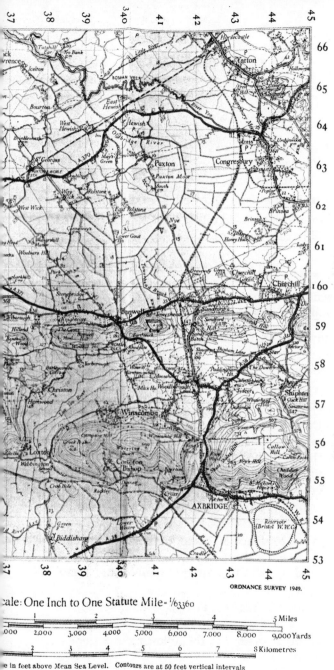

ORDNANCE SURVEY 1949.

GEOGRAPHY

PAPER I

(Two hours and a quarter allowed)

You will not be allowed to write during the first fifteen minutes. The time is to be spent in studying the questions and the accompanying maps and photograph.

Answer **four** questions. Question 1 is compulsory.

Where appropriate sketch-maps and diagrams should be used to illustrate answers.

SECTION A Map Interpretation

You are advised to spend not more than half an hour on this compulsory question.

1. Study the 1-in. Ordnance Survey map (*on pages 54–55*), the outline map, which is on a reduced scale, and the accompanying picture (*opposite*).

    Answer the following questions:

    (a) On the outline map: (i) mark the railway from Congresbury (C) to Axbridge (A); (ii) mark the height of the contour line shown and shade all the land above that height; (iii) mark clearly and use the given letters to indicate the position of one example of each of the following: coastal cliffs (w), a meander (x), a ferry-route (y), an artificial stretch of river (z).

    (b) What evidence provided on the Ordnance Survey map shows that: (i) lowland X may be liable to flooding, (ii) the main highlands are of a pervious rock?

    (c) Study the picture of Crook Peak (387559) taken from the east and, with the aid of the map, answer the following questions.

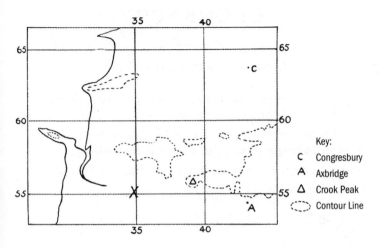

Key:

C Congresbury
A Axbridge
△ Crook Peak
◌ Contour Line

CROOK PEAK FROM THE EAST

   (i) Name the village shown in the distance
      and the farm in the right-hand foreground.

  (ii) Name the two hills between Crook Peak
      and the view-point.

 (iii) Give the six-figure map reference number
      of the point from which you consider the
      photograph was taken.

(d) State briefly the factors which you think have
influenced the position of Loxton village.

SECTION B The British Isles

At least **two** questions must be attempted in this section.

2. (a) On the given population map of Wales (*opposite*):

   (i) *print* the words slate, coal, water-supply,
      holiday resort, where these are most important

  (ii) mark and name Cardiff, Swansea, Holyhead,
      the Pembroke peninsula

(b) (i) Why is sheep-rearing important in the interior
of Wales?

  (ii) What has given rise to the high density of
population in some of the valleys of South
Wales?

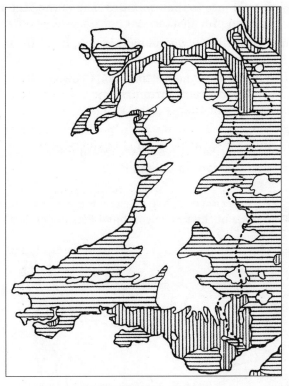

PERSONS PER Sq. MILE

 UNDER 50   50-250   OVER 250

3. With reference to the simplified map of the Midlands of England provided (*below*):

  (*a*) Name (i) the two upland areas A, B, (ii) the two lowland areas C, D

  (*b*) mark and name Nottingham, Crewe, Stoke-on-Trent, Birmingham

  (*c*) shade and name two coalfields

  (*d*) *Either*

   (i) describe the main features of the natural landscape of upland B

   or

   (ii) describe and give reasons for the importance of *one* of the towns you have marked on the map

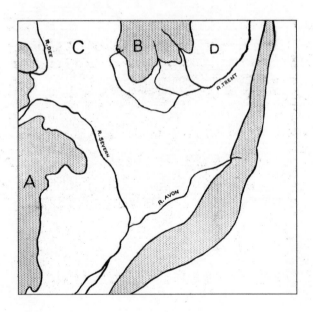

4. (*a*) On the outline map of the British Isles (*below*), which shows area B with a small temperature range and area A with a greater temperature range, mark and name

   (i) 40°F mean January isotherm and 60°F mean July isotherm

   (ii) approximate mean annual rainfall at each of S and W

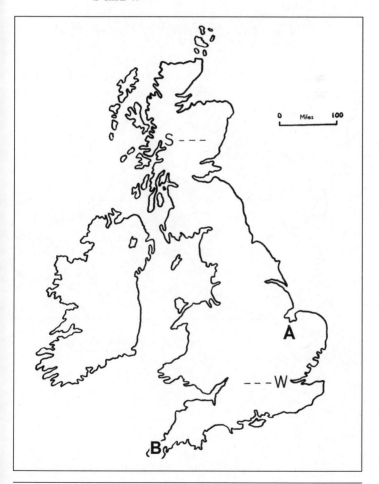

(*b*) In your answer book explain

    (i) why the range of temperature is greater at A than B

    (ii) why the mean annual rainfall at W is less than at S

    (iii) how and why the farming at A differs from that at B

5. (*a*) On the map of the Home Counties (*below*)

    (i) **Name two** of the rivers and **three** of the

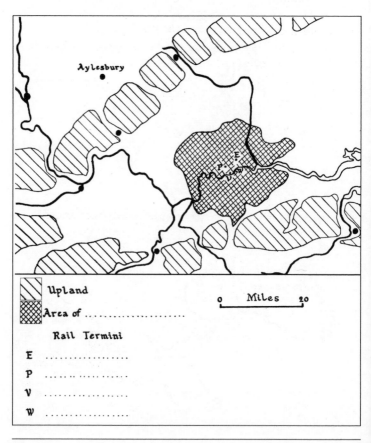

Aylesbury

Upland

Area of ....

Rail Termini

E   ....

P   ....

V   ....

W   ....

0   Miles   20

towns marked by dots; (ii) print North Downs and Chilterns each in an appropriate place; (iii) complete the key, (iv) draw lines to show the courses, from their London termini, of **one** railway route to the north and **one** railway route to the south and in each case **name** the gap followed and indicate the chief destination.

(b) Describe and account for (i) the manufacturing industries of inner London and (ii) the manufacturing industries on the outskirts of London.

6. Under headings (a) relief, (b) climate and (c) occupations, state similarities between the coasts of west Scotland and of the south-west peninsula of England.

7. Give geographical reasons to account for the considerable emphasis on

   (a) manufacturing industries in the Central Lowlands of Scotland

   (b) pastoral farming in Eire

8. The population of East Anglia is evenly distributed whereas the population of the Lake District is concentrated in a few areas.

   Expand this statement and suggest geographical reasons to explain it.

Ref: 280/1 AQA (AEB) Q1, 2, 3 1955; Q5, 6 1957; Q7, 8 1958; Q4 1959

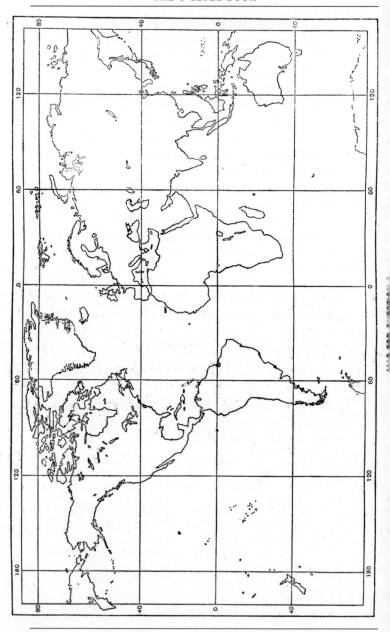

GEOGRAPHY

PAPER II

(Two hours and a quarter allowed)

You will not be allowed to write during the first fifteen minutes. The time is to be spent in studying the questions and the accompanying maps.

Answer **four** questions – **one** question from Section A and **three** from Section B.

Where appropriate sketch-maps and diagrams should be used to illustrate answers.

SECTION A General Physical Geography of the World

Answer **one** question from this section.

1. (a) On the outline map of the world provided (*opposite*):

   (i) mark in with a cross (X) the position 40°N, 90°W

   (ii) draw a line joining the places which have the sun overhead at noon on 21st June and write on the line 'sun overhead'

   (iii) mark in with an arrow the direction of the summer Monsoon winds along the West Coast of India and write the letter 'M' near the arrow

   (iv) draw the 32°F sea-level January isotherm for the North Atlantic Ocean and write '32°F' on the line

   (v) mark with an arrow the direction of flow of a cool ocean current in the Southern hemisphere and name it 'cool current'

   (b) On the outline map mark and indicate by means of the letters given in the brackets each of the following features: the Pampas (A), a range of young fold mountains in the *southern continents* (B), the Prairies of Canada (C), a rift-valley lake (D), an extensive stretch of coral reef (E), a fjord coast (F), the Kalahari desert (G).

(c) (i) Describe clearly the climate of *either* the Pampas *or* the Prairies

 (ii) Explain what is meant by *either* a rift-valley lake *or* a coral reef

2. Write a simple account to explain:

 (a) Why noon-shadows shorten and days get longer in the early summer in the British Isles

 (b) Why, at breakfast time in England, one can listen to a broadcast from Australia of the closing period of a test match taking place there

3. Describe briefly the *physical* features you would expect to see in the following areas and locate an example of each area:

 (a) an alluvial plain drained by the lower course of a river

 (b) a cliff coastline where there is active erosion in progress

 (c) a young folded mountain region with snowfields and valley glaciers

4. Expand and explain the following statements, each of which concerns places *on approximately the same latitude or longitude*.

 (a) The mean monthly temperature at Quito (Ecuador) differs by over 20°F from that of Manaos (Brazil)

 (b) The annual range of temperature at Vancouver is 27°F whereas that at Winnipeg is 69°F

 (c) The January temperature for Archangel (USSR) is 7°F while that for Port Sudan (Sudan) is 74°F

SECTION B

Answer **three** questions from this section.

5. (a) On the simple sketch-map provided (*below*) mark
   and name: Tibet, Bombay, Singapore, Colombo,
   Burma.

   (b) Explain why irrigation is necessary in parts of
   India and Pakistan, marking two areas of
   irrigation on the map provided. Choose *one* of
   these areas and describe briefly the methods of
   irrigation which are used.

   (c) Name one food crop and one raw material
   produced in any of the countries shown on the map
   and describe briefly the conditions under which
   each is produced.

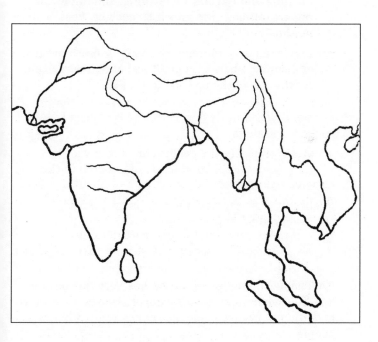

6. Explain why, as a student of Geography, you associate:

   (a) the 'Mediterranean' regions with fruit and wine

   (b) the African Savannas with 'Big Game'

   (c) Merino sheep with Australia

7. The great forests of Africa differ from those of Siberia in type, conditions of growth, kind of timber and methods used for obtaining it. Briefly state how they differ as regards:

   (a) location and climate

   (b) type of tree and timber produced

   (c) methods of handling the timber

8. (a) Explain the meaning of the terms **intensive** farming and **extensive** farming, and name one important food crop grown by each of these methods.

   (b) Locate an area (outside Europe) for **each** method of farming where it is practised and give reasons for the use of the method in that area.

9. For **each** of tea in Ceylon, cotton in southern USA, rubber in Malaya

   (a) state, precisely, the geographical conditions necessary for the production of the crop in the given area.

   (b) briefly describe how the crop is grown and prepared for export.

10. Explain why the lower Nile valley with little natural vegetation is densely populated, the plain of the Amazon with ample vegetation has very few people and Southern Siberia with a natural vegetation which is neither very dense nor scanty has relatively few people.

11. Give reasons to account for the concentration of population in *three* of the following areas: northern Italy, south-eastern Brazil, the higher land in Peru and Ecuador, the St Lawrence Lowlands and Lake Peninsula.

12. (*a*) Explain the term 'soil erosion'.

    (*b*) Name and locate three widely separated areas where it occurs.

    (*c*) Describe the causes of soil erosion and the methods which may be taken to counteract and prevent it.

Ref: 280/2 AQA (AEB) Q1, 2, 5, 6 1955; Q3, 4, 7 1956; Q8, 9 1957; Q10 1958; Q11, 12 1959

HOUSEHOLD COOKERY

PAPER I

(Two hours allowed)

Answer **four** questions: **one** from Section A and **three** from Section B.

You are advised to spend about 40 minutes on Section A.

SECTION A

Answer **one** question from this section.

1. (*a*) What is the reason for the nutritive importance of eggs in a diet? Give reasons for the statements you make.

   (*b*) List the main purposes for which eggs are used in cookery and give an example of each one mentioned.

2. (*a*) List the food substances necessary to maintain good health and explain the nutritive value of each.

   (*b*) What food groups are represented in milk, butter, carrots, oatmeal, and jam?

SECTION B

Answer **three** questions from this section.

3. Give clear instructions for the preparation and cooking of:

   (*a*) a cabbage

   (*b*) a baked egg custard

   (*c*) a white coating sauce

   Give reasons for the statements you make.

4. (a) What faults in the preparation and/or cooking could cause the following:

    (i) greasy flavourless stew

    (ii) an unset cornflour mould

    (iii) heavy scones

  (b) How can these faults be avoided?

5. (a) Name the factors on which success depends in the making and baking of shortcrust pastry.

  (b) Explain the effect of oven heat on the ingredients used in the pastry.

6. What are the main points to consider when making and steaming a pudding using the creaming method?

7. (a) State the kind of fat you would use for *each* of the following:

    (i) a boiled fruit pudding

    (ii) rough puff pastry

    (iii) a white sauce

    (iv) a gingerbread

    (v) queen cakes

  (b) Describe fully the method of adding the fat to the other ingredients in any *three* of these instances.

Ref: 200/1 AQA (AEB) Q1, 3, 6 1955; Q2, 4, 5 1956; Q7 1957

HOUSEHOLD COOKERY

PAPER II

(Two hours allowed)

Answer **four** questions: **one** from Section A and **three** from Section B.

You are advised to spend about 40 minutes on Section A.

SECTION A

Answer **one** question from this section.

1. (*a*) Name the food constituents found in milk and explain the nutritive value of each.

   (*b*) How can a housewife ensure that her milk supply keeps in good condition in hot weather?

2. (*a*) Explain the nutritive value of green vegetables and state how this may be reduced by carelessness in the preparation and cooking.

   (*b*) What is meant by conservative cooking?

SECTION B

Answer **three** questions from this section.

3. (*a*) Describe how to make batter and how to cook it by *two* different methods.

   (*b*) What are the points on which success depends when making batter?

4. Explain the meaning of **five** of the following cookery terms and give **one** instance of the use of each: simmer; sauté; clarify (fat); steaming; au gratin; batter; and purée.

5. (*a*) Give the proportions of the ingredients used for the making of a white flowing sauce.

(*b*) Name **three** ways in which this sauce may be varied and a dish with which each may be served.

(*c*) What faults may occur in the making of a white sauce using a roux and how may they be avoided?

6. Why are the following practices in cookery important:

   (*a*) frying the meat for a brown stew

   (*b*) sieving flour

   (*c*) grating cheese

   (*d*) heating fat correctly before frying

   (*e*) using warm ingredients for bread making

7. Why are protein foods important? In each case name **three** examples of those which could be included in the diet of (i) a vegetarian; (ii) a farm worker; and (iii) an elderly lady.

Ref: 200/1 AQA (AEB) Q1, 3, 6 1957; Q2, 4, 5, 7 1958

MUSIC

PAPER I

(Two hours allowed)

All candidates must attempt Section A and **one** of the Sections B (i) to (vi). Candidates should not devote longer than **one** hour to Section A.

SECTION A

Answer Question 1 and **two** others from this section.

Wherever possible, questions should be illustrated by appropriate music quotations.

1. Write down the following compositions in chronological order (to save time, you may refer to each composition by its number):

    (i)   Peter and the Wolf (Prokovief)

    (ii) Now is the month of maying (Morley)

    (iii) The 'Enigma' Variations (Elgar)

    (iv) The Mastersingers (Wagner)

    (v)   Who is Sylvia? (Schubert)

    (vi) The 'Surprise' Symphony (Haydn)

    (vii) The Little Sweep (Britten)

    (viii) The incidental music to A Midsummer Night's Dream (Mendelssohn)

    (ix) Messiah (Handel)

    (x)   Nymphs and Shepherds (Purcell)

2. What kinds of music and musical instruments might have been found in an educated English household in the first twenty-five years of the seventeenth century?

---

3. Explain why the music of Berlioz, Schumann and Dvorak is described as *romantic*.

4. Why is Henry Purcell regarded as one of the most important of English composers?

5. What is meant by saying that the style of Bach and Handel is polyphonic? Illustrate your answer by reference to suitable works.

6. State what you understand by the term *oratorio* by reference to typical examples. Explain how an oratorio differs from an opera.

7. Carl Phillip Emmanuel Bach has been called the 'father' of the symphony. What composers followed him in this field until the death of Schubert? Imagine you are taking an interested friend, who has not heard such a piece before, to hear a sonata or a symphony of your choice. What background information would you give him about sonatas and symphonies in general to help him to enjoy it?

SECTION B

PART (i) – The Structure of Music

PART (ii) – Keyboard Music

PART (iii) – European Song

PART (iv) – The Orchestra

PART (v) – The Smaller Orchestral Combinations

PART (vi) – Choral Music

Answer **three** questions **all chosen from one part** of this section. The title of the part from which your questions are chosen must be clearly indicated.

Quote music examples wherever possible.

PART (i) – The Structure of Music

1. In what respect do rounds, canons and fugues resemble one another and in what way do they differ? Name *one* example of each and write out any *one* round.

2. What kinds of compositions are said to be written in contrapuntal style? Write brief notes on *one* example and illustrate your answer with quotations.

3. What do you understand by 'Minuet and Trio' form? Name and quote from any example with which you are familiar.

4. How do the Concertos of Bach and his contemporaries differ from those of Beethoven and later composers?

5. Give a description of the *aria da capo* form.

PART (ii) – Keyboard Music

1. What keyboard instruments have been in use from the sixteenth century to the present day? Give a short account of the chief characteristics of each one.

2. Give the names of some of the pieces of keyboard music by Robert Schumann. How do they differ from the works of Handel?

3. Name some of the types of composition which Bach wrote for the organ, quoting themes where possible.

4. How does a Scherzo in a Beethoven sonata differ from any of the Scherzos of Chopin?

5. What are the essential differences in the methods of tone production of the harpsichord and the modern pianoforte? How did Beethoven and later composers employ the new effects which the pianoforte made available to them?

PART (iii) – European Song

1. How did Schubert and his successors use the pianoforte accompaniment to add to the effectiveness of their songs? Illustrate your answer.

2. What is the meaning of the term *song cycle*? Illustrate your answer by reference to an example.

3. What were the most usual types of solo vocal music in the seventeenth and eighteenth centuries?

4. Write brief notes on the contribution made by any *two* of the following composers to the art of song writing:

   Wolf: Schumann: Mendelssohn: Warlock: Stanford.

Or

5. Describe the contribution made by any *two* of the following composers to the art of song writing:

   Schubert: Dowland: Parry: Brahms

PART (iv) – The Orchestra

1. (a) Make a list of the brass wind instruments usually found in a modern orchestra.

   (b) Describe very briefly how the sound is produced and how notes of different pitch are produced in each case.

2. (a) Name the various instruments in the string orchestra and indicate for each instrument its tuning and lowest note.

   (b) Explain: pizzicato; arco; con sordino; double-stopping.

3. What were the functions of the harpsichord player in orchestral music of the first half of the eighteenth century? Why is the harpsichord player not necessary in modern orchestral music?

4. In Bach's works for orchestra there is a part called Continuo. Explain the purpose of the continuo in such music.

5. What additional instruments have been introduced into the symphony orchestra since Beethoven's death? Who were the composers who made use of these instruments?

PART (v) – The Smaller Orchestral Combinations

1. Chamber music as we understand it can be fairly said to date from Haydn's day. In what ways does it differ from the domestic music of the sixteenth and seventeenth centuries?

2. The orchestra has undergone many changes since the time of Haydn, but one chamber music combination has remained the same since then. What is this combination? Give a short account of the development of its repertory from Haydn to Schubert.

3. What instruments are found in a Recorder Consort? Write down the lowest-sounding note for each instrument.

4. In the early seventeenth century, music was published as 'Apt for the viols and voices'. What does this tell us about early string consort music? Mention some of the composers who wrote such music and give an account of the viol family of instruments.

5. What was the essential difference between the use of the harpsichord in the instrumental works of Corelli and the use of the pianoforte in a Haydn pianoforte trio?

PART (vi) – Choral Music

1. Describe the different forms of choral music and music for vocal ensembles which were in existence between 1550 and 1625.

2. What part did the *chorale* play in the church music of Germany? Illustrate your answer by reference to the music of J.S. Bach.

3. What was Mendelssohn's contribution to choral music?

4. What has been the role of the Chapel Royal and the cathedral choirs in England in fostering choral music from medieval times to the present century? Mention some of the outstanding musicians connected with either the Chapel Royal or a cathedral choir.

5. What is a madrigal? Name some representative examples and their composers.

Ref: 420/2 AQA (AEB) Section A Q1, 2, 5 1957; Q6, 7 1958; Q3, 4 1959; Section B (i) 1, (ii) 2, (ii) 3, (ii) 5, (iii) 4, (iv) 1, (iv) 2, (iv) 3, (v) 1, (v) 3, (vi) 4, (vi) 5, 1957; (i) 2, (i) 3, (i) 4, (ii) 4, (iv) 4, (iv) 5, (v) 2, (v) 4, (v) 5 1958; (i) 5, (ii) 1, (iii) 1, 2, 3, 5, (vi) 1, 2, 3 1959

USEFUL
REFERENCE MATERIAL

FORMULAE

$$\text{Speed} = \frac{\text{Distance}}{\text{Time}}$$

$$\text{Density} = \frac{\text{Mass}}{\text{Volume}}$$

$$\text{Force} = \text{Pressure} \times \text{Area}$$

$$\text{Area of a circle} = \pi r^2$$

$$\text{Volume of sphere:} \ \frac{4}{3} \ \pi r^3$$

$$\text{Volume of cone:} \ \frac{1}{3} \ \pi r^2 h$$

Pythagoras' Theorem for right-angled triangles:
$$a^2 + b^2 = c^2$$

Periodic Table of the Elements

1	2	3	4	5	6	7	8	9	10	11	12	13	14	15	16	17	18
hydrogen 1 **H** 1.0079																	helium 2 **He** 4.0026
lithium 3 **Li** 6.941	beryllium 4 **Be** 9.0122											boron 5 **B** 10.811	carbon 6 **C** 12.01	nitrogen 7 **N** 14.007	oxygen 8 **O** 15.999	fluorine 9 **F** 18.998	neon 10 **Ne** 20.180
sodium 11 **Na** 22.990	magnesium 12 **Mg** 24.305											aluminium 13 **Al** 26.982	silicon 14 **Si** 28.086	phosphorus 15 **P** 30.974	sulfur 16 **S** 32.065	chlorine 17 **Cl** 35.453	argon 18 **Ar** 39.948
potassium 19 **K** 39.098	calcium 20 **Ca** 40.078	scandium 21 **Sc** 44.956	titanium 22 **Ti** 47.867	vanadium 23 **V** 50.942	chromium 24 **Cr** 51.996	manganese 25 **Mn** 54.938	iron 26 **Fe** 55.845	cobalt 27 **Co** 58.933	nickel 28 **Ni** 58.693	copper 29 **Cu** 63.546	zinc 30 **Zn** 65.39	gallium 31 **Ga** 69.723	germanium 32 **Ge** 72.61	arsenic 33 **As** 74.922	selenium 34 **Se** 78.96	bromine 35 **Br** 79.904	krypton 36 **Kr** 83.80
rubidium 37 **Rb** 85.468	strontium 38 **Sr** 87.62	yttrium 39 **Y** 88.906	zirconium 40 **Zr** 91.224	niobium 41 **Nb** 92.906	molybdenum 42 **Mo** 95.94	technetium 43 **Tc** [98]	ruthenium 44 **Ru** 101.07	rhodium 45 **Rh** 102.91	palladium 46 **Pd** 106.42	silver 47 **Ag** 107.87	cadmium 48 **Cd** 112.41	indium 49 **In** 114.82	tin 50 **Sn** 118.71	antimony 51 **Sb** 121.76	tellurium 52 **Te** 127.60	iodine 53 **I** 126.90	xenon 54 **Xe** 131.29
caesium 55 **Cs** 132.91	barium 56 **Ba** 137.33	57-70 *	lutetium 71 **Lu** 174.97	hafnium 72 **Hf** 178.49	tantalum 73 **Ta** 180.95	tungsten 74 **W** 183.84	rhenium 75 **Re** 186.21	osmium 76 **Os** 190.23	iridium 77 **Ir** 192.22	platinum 78 **Pt** 195.08	gold 79 **Au** 196.97	mercury 80 **Hg** 200.59	thallium 81 **Tl** 204.38	lead 82 **Pb** 207.2	bismuth 83 **Bi** 208.98	polonium 84 **Po** [209]	astatine 85 **At** [210]	radon 86 **Rn** [222]
francium 87 **Fr** [223]	radium 88 **Ra** [226]	89-102 **	lawrencium 103 **Lr** [262]	rutherfordium 104 **Rf** [261]	dubnium 105 **Db** [262]	seaborgium 106 **Sg** [266]	bohrium 107 **Bh** [264]	hassium 108 **Hs** [269]	meitnerium 109 **Mt** [268]	ununnilium 110 **Uun** [271]	unununium 111 **Uuu** [272]	ununbium 112 **Uub** [277]	ununquadium 114 **Uuq** [289]					

*Lanthanide series

lanthanum 57 **La** 138.91	cerium 58 **Ce** 140.12	praseodymium 59 **Pr** 140.91	neodymium 60 **Nd** 144.24	promethium 61 **Pm** [145]	samarium 62 **Sm** 150.36	europium 63 **Eu** 151.96	gadolinium 64 **Gd** 157.25	terbium 65 **Tb** 158.93	dysprosium 66 **Dy** 162.50	holmium 67 **Ho** 164.93	erbium 68 **Er** 167.26	thulium 69 **Tm** 168.93	ytterbium 70 **Yb** 173.04

**Actinide series

actinium 89 **Ac** [227]	thorium 90 **Th** 232.04	protactinium 91 **Pa** 231.04	uranium 92 **U** 238.03	neptunium 93 **Np** [237]	plutonium 94 **Pu** [244]	americium 95 **Am** [243]	curium 96 **Cm** [247]	berkelium 97 **Bk** [247]	californium 98 **Cf** [251]	einsteinium 99 **Es** [252]	fermium 100 **Fm** [257]	mendelevium 101 **Md** [258]	nobelium 102 **No** [259]

ANSWERS

ENGLISH LANGUAGE

PAPER 1

1. (*a*) To include the following points:
London bus services have been reduced by 5 per cent;
country buses have regular customers but town buses
have greater competition from other modes of transport;
buses have more frequent stopping places, but are
hindered by traffic congestion and high fares; in London,
more people are using the underground, walking or
cycling; buses remain crowded at peak times but it
would not be cost effective to provide more crews for the
whole day; other towns are likely to follow suit and
reduce services; perhaps a lowering of fares is the only
solution.

(*b*)   (i) characteristic or indicative of
    (ii) active, robust, powerful in effect
   (iii) become inferior in quality
   (iv) when demand is greatest, busiest
    (v) overcrowding on the road, traffic jams
   (vi) necessary, indispensable

(*c*)   (i) a railway line that leads off from and connects to a
main railway line, linking smaller towns rather
than cities
    (ii) a railway line that connects the suburban locations
of a town or city
   (iii) the people who work on the buses
   (iv) a bicycle with a chargeable motor for increased
speed

(*d*)   (i) the Executive is a single person, and so the
apostrophe comes before the 's' to denote
possession, i.e. the decision of the London
Transport Executive
    (ii) the apostrophe is placed after the 's' to indicate
that there is more than one crew, i.e. the dislike of
the bus crews

(*e*) The semi-colon splits the sentence into two parts of equal
sense in the same way that a conjunction would do.

(*f*) The word station is not normally associated with bus
routes, and is being used to refer to unofficial main

stopping places equivalent to those fixed stations a train stops at.

2. (a)   (i)   newly grown
      (ii)   recently laid
     (iii)   unspoilt and unpreserved
     (iv)   clean and awake
      (v)   recently applied
     (vi)   cold, brisk
    (vii)   cool and refreshing, free from impurities
   (viii)   not saline, pure
     (ix)   recent, additional
      (x)   youthful and healthy

(b)   (i)   an informal agreement that is binding as a matter of personal honour
     (ii)   a person who unwittingly or maliciously depresses/discourages someone while attempting to console them
    (iii)   an epic battle or conflict; a struggle of enormous magnitude
    (iv)   resembling a parent in appearance or behaviour
     (v)   very seldom, rarely
    (vi)   actions are more important than appearances
   (vii)   to do something pointless and superfluous

3. (a) immature, dissimilar, ignoble, illegible, irrational, incomplete

(b) vocal, creditable, spectacular, laborious, beneficial, exemplary

(c)   (i)   The milkman finished his round.
     (ii)   That is her mother.
    (iii)   As you are oldest, you can go first.
    (iv)   Each painting was beautiful.
     (v)   He ran off.
    (vi)   Shakespeare coined many words.

4. (a)   (i)   Uncle Tom has agreed to share his money between you and me.
     (ii)   The dog had hurt its paw.
     (ii)   The number of accidents on the road is increasing.
     (ii)   While she was crossing the road, her heel got stuck in a manhole cover.

(b) Olympian – majestic, grand; pasteurization – partial

sterilization of a substance, e.g. milk, to destroy harmful micro-organisms; Martian – an inhabitant of Mars; titanic – of enormous strength and size; tantalizing – something that evokes interest and excitement; Elizabethan – relating to Elizabeth I, or referring to the period of her rule.

PAPER II

1. (a) To include the following points:
   The guilds were run according to an intricate code of conduct; they served to protect both craftsmen and the public, ensuring the quality of goods, eradicating counterfeits and controlling prices; 'searchers' visited craftsmen to inspect goods and pricing; wardens ensured those breaching the codes were punished; the guilds had a monopoly of their trades meaning that non-members were unable to succeed but that members were honest and produced quality goods; chaplains of the guilds encouraged teamwork through events, fundraising, and building work; because of the existence of the guilds, most craftsman worked hard, otherwise they risked being expelled.

   (b) an organization designed to protect its members and maintain high standards

   (c) Through monopolizing the trade, the guild ensured its members were free from competition from outsiders and foreigners and inspired in them a desire to produce high-quality workmanship.

   (d) *ruthlessly* without pity, unrelentingly; *askance* with distrust; *spiritual* devotional/sacred; *beneficence* goodness; *lore* knowledge

   (e) Customs are the traditional mores of a group of people. Beliefs are the set of ideas accepted by an individual or group of people to be true. Customs are conventionally founded on beliefs.

2. (a) *a square deal* a fair agreement; *a square meal* a substantial meal; *a square dance* a form of traditional dance in which the couples form squares; *to square a person* to secure the help or compliance of, often by offering reward; *to square an account* to balance the

books; *to square accounts* to reconcile, even or settle a matter.

(b) an almoner distributes alms for an institution; a psychiatrist is a physician who specializes in mental health; a geologist is a scientist who studies the earth and its formation; a journalist reports, writes or broadcasts news stories; an accountant inspects or audits a person or company's financial accounts; a draughtsman is an artist specializing in mechanical drawings.

3. (a) (i) credible; (ii) infallible; (iii) incompatible; (iv) visible; (v) inedible; (vi) illegible

   (b) Licence: James Bond has a licence to kill.
License: I license you to practise law.
Eliminate: I sprayed perfume to eliminate the odour.
Illuminate: If we light the candles, we will illuminate the garden.
Inform: He promised to inform me when he had arrived.
Conform: She will never conform to the rules of society.
Official: We are attending the official opening of the town hall.
Officious: His officious interference left me feeling stifled.

4. (a) (i) As soon as we have laid her new carpet she will give us her old one.
     (ii) The player was dropped because he disagreed with his captain.
     (iii) He ended his letter with 'Yours sincerely' rather than 'Yours faithfully'.

   (b) A cup: a small, open drinking vessel that is often made of china.
A saucer: a small, shallow dish on which a cup rests.
A jug: a vessel used for holding liquids, often with a handle and lipped edge for pouring.
A plate: a flat, usually circular piece of crockery on which food is served.
A spoon: a utensil used for mixing, serving and eating food.
A knife: a utensil with a blade edge for cutting food.

MATHEMATICS

PAPER I

1. (a) 18.84
   (b) 18.75
   (c) XBD = 105°; BDX = 30°; BXD = 45°

2. (a) b = 2 (A/h) − a
   (b) $\cos A = \frac{12}{13}$ $\sin (180° - A) = \frac{5}{13}$

3. (a) y = 5
   (b) (i) 1.12in. (to 2 dp)
       (ii) 83.62° (to 2 dp)

4. (a) (2x − 1) (3x + 5)
   (b) x = 1.3 or x = − 0.3
   (c) $\frac{100 (q - p)}{p}$

5. (a) 58.4
   (b) x = 5.625
   (c) BXC = 30°

6. 1.9in. (+ or − 0.1in.)

7. CAB = 67° (+ or − 0.1°)

8. 44.5%; 21 weeks.

9. (i) 66cm²
   (ii) 6.6cm
   (iii) ABC = 36.9°; ACB = 30.5°; BAC = 112.6° (all to 1 dp)

10. (a) x = 1.64 or x = − 2.14
    (b) 8.9%

PAPER II

1. (a) (3x + 5) (x − 4)
   (b) 59°F
   (c) y = − 2, x = 3

2. (a) x = −1.5 or x = 2
   (b) 104cm²

3. (a) a(y + 3a) (2y − 5); (b) x = −2 or x = $\frac{1}{3}$; (c) 24cm; 120cm²

4. (a) 11.25   (b) 8.5

   (c) DAC = 58°; ACD = 58°; ADC = 64°

5. (a) $\frac{m(b+g)-nb}{g}$

   (b) 240

   (c) 4.76in.; 28.45in.

6. $y = 2x + \frac{80}{x}$; 16 in batch

7. 8mm

8. 2.6cm (+ or – 0.1cm)

9. 270mph

10. $\frac{3}{10}$ or 0.3in.

PAPER III

1. (a) y = 2 or 4, x = $\frac{3}{2}$ or 2

   (b) 10.56 (to 2 dp)

2. 82.50 ft; 54.79° (to 2 dp)

3. (a) 1.72

   (b) 15

4. Area = $\frac{32}{3}$ or 10.67; Volume = $\frac{512}{15}$ π or 107.25 (to 2 dp)

5. (i) 101.85 (to 2 dp)

   (ii) 3.51 (to 2 dp)

6. (a) x = 1.59 or x = –1.26

   (b) x = 2 or $\frac{2}{3}$, y = 1 or $-1\frac{2}{3}$

7. 1.22 (to 2 dp)

8. Angle C = 75.5°; XY = 3.56cm

9. 40mm

10. $\frac{BQ}{AP} = \frac{AP}{CR}$ because quadrilaterals BQAP and PARC are similar.

GENERAL SCIENCE

PAPER I A

1. (a) 1000ft per second (the sound takes 2 seconds to travel 2000ft to and from the cliff)
   (b) 4.73 miles (to 2 dp)

2. (a) steel
      Reason: the atoms in steel stay permanently aligned to form poles once magnetized.
   (b) soft iron
      Reason: the atoms are only aligned when an electric current is flowing through it.

3. (a) Mixture
   (b) Nitrogen, oxygen, inert gases (mainly argon) and carbon dioxide
   (c) 78 per cent nitrogen, 21 per cent oxygen

4. (a) Sodium hydroxide + hydrogen
   (b) Calcium oxide + carbon dioxide
   (c) Calcium hydroxide

5. (a) It will grow (bend) towards the light.
   (b) They will turn towards the light.
   (c) They will grow (bend) away from the light.

6. A = enamel; B = dentine; C = pulp; D = cementum

7. (a) straight; one; refraction
   (b) It makes the pond appear shallower as the light rays seem to come to our eyes from a higher point

8. Common salt = Sodium Chloride = $NaCl$
   Washing soda = Sodium Carbonate = Na_2CO_3
   Quicklime = Calcium Oxide = CaO

9. (a) (i) hydrogen
       (ii) basic/alkaline
      (iii) blue; red
   (b) Examples include nitric acid, hydrochloric acid, acetic acid

10. (a) The sodium melts and moves on the surface on a cushion of hydrogen gas. The gas may self-ignite.
    (b) A white precipitate forms.
    (c) A white precipitate forms at first but dissolves and the solution becomes transparent again.

11. (a) (i) The main site of photosynthesis
        (ii) Contains stomata for exchange of gases and transpiration
    (b) (i) Absorbs nutrients and water
        (ii) Anchors plants in soil

LIGHT ENERGY

12. Carbon dioxide + water $\rightarrow$ glucose (starch) + oxygen

13. Warm blood; bear live young; suckle young

14. It is a good conductor of heat; it expands a large amount for each degree in temperature; it is an opaque and easy to view liquid.

15. 75g water would have a maximum temperature of 40°C.

16. (a)

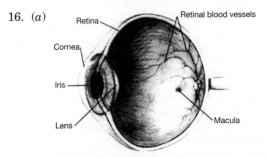

    (b) Short sight, or myopia, is an eye condition caused by the inability of the lens to focus light from distant objects on to the retina. Distant objects therefore appear blurred. The condition can be corrected by wearing glasses containing a concave lens that diverges the light rays so that they focus on the retina.

17. (a) Soap reacts with calcium and/or magnesium salts in hard water to form scum. Only when all the hardness has reacted will the soap lather and emulsify dirt. Rainwater is soft because it has no dissolved salts from rocks.

(b)　(i) A mixture of two liquids, one dispersed as droplets in the other.
　　(ii) Fats are emulsified by bile in the duodenum.
　　(iii) Bile is produced in the liver and stored in the gall bladder.

18. (a) Water, urea, creatinine, uric acid, salts
　　(b) Urine is formed in the kidneys due to the ultrafiltration of blood to remove waste materials for excretion from the bladder. Useful materials and water are reabsorbed into the blood.
　　(c)　(i) Using a pH meter or Universal Indicator
　　　　(ii) Add a silver nitrate solution. A white precipitate indicates chlorides.

19. (a) A concave mirror used close to the teeth will give a magnified image. It is warmed to stop condensation from forming on it from breath.
　　(b) The electric lamp produces very little blue light compared to daylight. The pigment in the flower reflects red and blue light to the eyes but in the absence of blue light it will only reflect red, and therefore will appear red.
　　(c) The shoots of the plant are phototropic, i.e. they grow towards the light. Rotating the plant will ensure that if the shoots bend one way this can be corrected so that they grow straight.

20. (a) Bacteria grow in plaque on the teeth. Plaque forms mainly due to eating sugary foods. The bacteria convert the sugar to acids. Acids destroy tooth enamel that leads to holes in the tooth and decay.
　　(b) Bacteria in milk break down milk sugar (lactose) to form lactic acid that makes the milk taste sour. The acid always coagulates protein in the milk to form the 'curds' associated with sour milk.
　　(c) Nitrogen fixing bacteria live in root nodules of leguminous plants. They can convert atmospheric nitrogen into nitrates that the plant uses to make proteins for growth and metabolism.
　　(d) Bacteria in a compost help biodegrade organic matter. When this happens the temperature rises and decomposition occurs quickly.

PAPER I B

1. (a) Yellow, (b) white (or pale grey), (c) white,
   (d) colourless

2. a) Copper metal and water, (b) a redox reaction, (c) the
   burning of a fossil fuel in air (carbon + oxygen = carbon
   dioxide)

3. E; C; M; C; E; C; M

4. (a) Sugar (glucose/fructose) →
       alcohol (ethanol) + carbon dioxide + water
   (b)   (i) Production of alcohol (ethanol)
        (ii) Raising bread dough

5. (a) Gastric juice, (b) the hydrolysis of the peptide bonds of
   proteins

6. (a) Bacteria in milk break down milk sugar (lactose)
       to form lactic acid which makes the milk taste sour.
       The acid always coagulates protein in the milk to form
       the 'curds' associated with sour milk.
   (b)   (i) Micro-organisms cannot grow without water.
        (ii) At low temperatures micro-organisms grow slowly.

7. From top to bottom: 2; 4; 1; 3; 5; 7

8. (a) Potential; kinetic
   (b) Heat (thermal); light
   (c) In the muscles
   (d) Stored chemical energy produced in respiration by the
       breakdown of glucose to form ATP

9. (a) Hydrogen
   (b) Hydrogen; oxygen; anode; 2; 1; platinum

10. (a) Incisors; canines; premolars and molars
    (b) Dentine

11. (a) A substance made from only one type of atom
    (b) Carbon, hydrogen, oxygen and nitrogen

12. (a) Stomata
    (b) Chlorophyll
    (c)   (i) CO_2 taken in for photosynthesis, O_2 out
         (ii) None: they are closed

13. (*a*) Atmospheric pressure
    (*b*) Relative humidity
    (*c*) Temperature

14. (*a*) (i) Potential difference
        (ii) Resistance
        (iii) Current intensity
    (*b*) Ohm's Law: $V = IR$

15. (*a*) Dilute sulphuric acid
    (*b*) Ammonium chloride solution
    (*c*) Acetylene
    (*d*) Methane

16. (*a*) The angle of incidence equals the angle of reflection; the incident ray, the reflected ray and the normal all lie in the same plane.
    (*b*) To verify the first law: using a ray box, shine a beam of light at an angle to a plane mirror. Mark the position of the reflected ray. Mark also the position of the mirror and draw the normal to the mirror at the point at which the ray is reflected. The angle between the incident ray and the normal will equal the angle between the reflected ray and the normal.

17. (*a*) Iron is a solid at room temperature; it has a high melting point; it conducts electricity and heat; it is strong and ductile; it is shiny; it is electropositive (forms ionic compounds). Nitrogen is a gas at room temperature; it has a low melting point; it forms covalent compounds; its oxide is water soluble.
    (*b*) Plants absorb from the soil due to the action of nitrifying bacteria as ammonia nitrates. Bacteria are also found in the root nodules of legumes. Animals obtain nitrogen by eating plants or other animals.

18. (*a*) This is the quantity of heat required to change ice to water without temperature change. To find its value: heat a known mass of ice with a heater of known power. Switch on the heater for a measured amount of time, e.g. 180s. To calculate:
    Heat supplied in 180s = Power of heater (J/s) × 180 = xJ

    $$\text{Latent heat of fusion} = \frac{x\text{J}}{\text{Mass of water formed from ice}}$$

(b) The latent heat of fusion of ice is high (340 J/g). This means that it takes a lot of heat to melt snow on a sunny day. Snow acts as a layer of insulation for the plants, protecting them from very cold temperatures at night. The temperature of snow is fairly constant at 0°C. Because of the high latent heat of fusion it does not melt away on warm days.

19. (a) When current flows in the electromagnet the soft iron armature is attracted. The hammer hits the gong but the circuit breaks at the screw. The electromagnet no longer attracts the armature. Contact is remade with the screw and the circuit is complete again. This cycle repeats when the bell push is depressed.

   (b)   (i)   Steel would become permanently magnetized
        (ii)   Plastic is not magnetic

20. (a) Acidified water in a Hoffman Voltameter. Electrolysis gives oxygen and hydrogen gases that can be tested.

   (b) Simple distillation. Water is boiled and steam condensed. Impurities are left in the boiling vessel.

PAPER II A

1. (a) A = earth; B = moon; C = sun
   (b) A = sun; B = moon; C = earth

2. (a) It contains a pigment which reflects red light into our eyes and absorbs blue and green
   (b) Black, because it absorbs blue light
   (c) To reflect heat and light

3. (a) Aluminium; (b) Aluminium; (c) Steel

4. (a) Carbon dioxide and water
   (b) Light and presence of chlorophyll
   (c) Starch and oxygen

5. A body response to a stimulus

6. Jupiter; Pluto; Mercury; Venus

7. (a) Amperes; (b) Ohms; (c) Volts

8. (a) Sodium chloride + water
   (b) Calcium chloride + carbon dioxide + water

   (c) Sodium carbonate + carbon dioxide + water

9. (a) less
   (b) (i) soluble; (ii) soluble; (iii) insoluble;
   (iv) soluble; (v) partly soluble; (vi) soluble;
   (vii) insoluble; (viii) insoluble

10. Carbon (coke); coal tar; coal gas; ammonia

11. (a) 1 = radicle; 2 = lateral root; 3 = plumule;
    4 = testa; 5 = cotyledons
    (b) Warmth and moisture

12. (a) Haemoglobin
    (b) Red blood cells
    (c) (i) It combines with oxygen to form oxyhaemoglobin.
        (ii) Oxyhaemoglobin dissociates to form haemoglobin
             and oxygen.

13. (a) Organic material in soil
    (b) Its breakdown provides nutrients
    (c) Denitrifying bacteria remove nitrogen, making soil
        infertile, and oxygen cannot reach plant roots

14. (a) A body immersed in a liquid is buoyed by a force equal
        to the weight of the displaced liquid.
    (b) Sea water is denser than fresh water. If a body is less
        dense than a liquid it will float.
    (c) (i) $4cm^3$
        (ii) $5g/cm^3$

15. (a) a vacuum; (b) 343 m/s; (c) eardrum; the ossicles; cochlea

16. (a) Convection is the form of heat transfer that occurs
        in liquids and gases. As particles collide heat energy
        is transferred. An increase in temperature increases
        the number of collisions due to the conversion of heat
        energy into kinetic energy. A simple experiment to
        illustrate this involves the use of a convection square
        full of water. One corner of the square is heated and
        potassium permanganate crystals are introduced at the
        top. As heat is transferred in the water it becomes less
        dense and is pushed round the square by denser cold
        water. A convection current is produced and this can be
        tracked by pink colouration coming from the crystals.

(b) Water vapour breathed out increases and temperature rises. There is also an increase in CO_2 levels. A coal fire can be used to set up a convection current so cooler air will be drawn into the room down a chimney or flue.

17. (a) Chalk and limestone consist of calcium salts. These salts are dissolved into rainwater which falls on them. Granite does not contain calcium salts.

(b) Temporary hard water contains dissolved calcium hydrogen carbonate. This can be removed by boiling. Permanent hardness is not removed by boiling. It is caused by dissolved calcium sulphate and can only be removed chemically, e.g. using an ion exchange column where sodium is substituted for calcium.

18. (a) Nitrogen 78%; oxygen 21% ; CO_2 and inert gases 1%

(b) All living things respire which means they use atmospheric oxygen to produce energy. They thus remove oxygen from the air. Plants also photosynthesize. In this process, oxygen is produced to offset respiration uses. In the same way CO_2 is used in photosynthesis but excreted in respiration. In photosynthesis CO_2 is incorporated into organic chemicals, i.e. starch. Saprophytes feed by absorbing dead organic matter and breaking it down to be recycled in the environment.

19. (a) The heart is a muscular pumping organ situated in the thorax. It consists of four chambers but the left and right sides are not joined. Oxygenated blood from the lungs enters the left side and deoxygenated blood from the body enters the right side. The lower chambers of the heart are called ventricles and they are the muscular pumping chambers, separated from the top chambers by valves. The heart is designed to pump deoxygenated blood to the lungs for oxygenation and to pump the oxygenated blood to the rest of the body.

(b) In the ventricles

20. (a) (i) The wire will glow red hot and may melt.
(ii) The solution loses blue colour, bubbles of gas are seen at the anode and copper metal is deposited on the cathode.

       (iii) The compass needle pointer will align with one end of the coil.

  (b)   (i) No difference.

       (ii) Events at electrodes will swap over.

     (iii) The compass needle pointer will turn to the opposite end of the coil.

PAPER II B

1. (a) 1000 Pa (Pascal); (b) 8N (Newtons)

2. (a) The current through a metal conductor is directly proportional to the potential difference across its ends if temperature is constant.
   (b) 1.2 amperes

3. (a) Water (moisture) and air; (b) Painting and galvanizing

4. Chalk, zinc and copper sulphate

5. (a) Hooke's Law – extension of a spring is proportional to the stretching force
   (b) The coal would weigh slightly more at the bottom of the pit. The weight is due to the force of gravity and this is greater nearer to the centre of the earth.

6. (a) (i) Alkali; (ii) Salt
   (b) It provides nitrogen for plant growth and is used on alkaline soils to lower the pH.

7. (a) The random movement of particles from where they are more concentrated to where they are less concentrated.
   (b) (i) Oxygen diffuses from the lungs to the blood
        (ii) Carbon dioxide diffuses from stomata into palisade cells

8. (a) Ohm; (b) Tungsten; (c) Armature;
   (d) Manganese dioxide; (e) Commutator; (f) Voltameter

9. (a) (i) Carbon; (ii) hydrogen, sulphur, oxygen; (iii) carbon, hydrogen, oxygen

   (b) (i) M; (ii) C; (iii) M

10. (a) Clinical; (b) Mercury; (c) To break the mercury column so the temperature can be read; (d) It is shaken; (e) The temperature is too high at 100°C; (f) 36.9°C

11. hairs; osmosis; stomata; transpiration; wilts

12. (a) (i) Glucose; (ii) amino acids; (iii) fatty acids and glycerol
    (b) In the duodenum

13. (a) Place a sample of food in Biuret reagent. A colour change from blue to purple indicates the presence of protein.
    (b) Meat, fish, eggs, beans, soy, dairy products, pulses, nuts and seeds

14. (a) Warmth and moisture
    (b) Low temperatures (chilling, freezing); drying (removal of water); addition of preservatives; curing, pickling or salting

15. (a) Between the mirror and its focus
    (b) Shaving mirror
    (c) A real image is one that can be produced on a screen and is formed by rays that pass through it. A virtual image seems to come from behind a mirror and is produced by rays that seem to come from it but do not pass through it.

16. (a) Pressure increases with depth. If the spout was lower, tea would pour out of it until the liquid level was below the spout, which would mean it could never be filled to the top.
    (b) Glass is a poor conductor of heat and a poor expander, so it endures stresses due to sudden heat that cause it to crack.
    (c) They fluff their feathers to trap air. This forms a boundary layer that is warmed by their bodies and insulates them.
    (d) A convection current is formed by the fire so that air circulates round the room. Fresh air is drawn down the chimney as hot gases rise in the room.

17. Green plants are autotrophs (self-feeders). They photosynthesize to make starch. They also absorb nitrates. Nitrogen is required to make proteins. Animals are heterotrophs (other-feeders). They must consume green plants and other animals to gain the nutrients they require. Saprophytes (now called saprotrophs) are decomposers. They

obtain nutrients by breaking down dead and decaying plants and animals using externally secreted enzymes. Fungi, bacteria and protists are saprotrophs. These inter-dependencies are illustrated by the carbon and nitrogen cycles.

18. (a) The formation of frost breaks up large soil particles so that more oxygen can penetrate. It makes soil more fertile and well drained.

(b) The enzymes which cause seeds to germinate work more quickly in the higher temperatures. More photosynthesis can occur because of higher light intensity so plants grow quickly.

(c) Sweat takes heat from the skin as it changes from a liquid to a vapour (latent heat of vaporization).

(d) At high altitudes oxygen concentrations are lower because air is thinner. Less oxygen diffuses from lungs to blood so oxygen cylinders are needed.

19. (a) Quicklime (calcium oxide) is made by heating limestone (calcium carbonate) to above 825°C in a process called calcination.

(b) (i) A violent exothermic reaction occurs and calcium hydroxide is formed (slaked lime).

(ii) The calcium hydroxide starts to dissolve in the water and a substance called limewater is formed (slaked lime reacts less violently with water than quicklime).

(c) Lime is used to increase the pH of soils that are too acid. It is also added to lakes to reduce the effects of acid rain and is a constituent of mortar and plaster.

20. The internal combustion engine has an internal combustion chamber, hence its name. The combustion chamber is a confined space in which a fuel and air are mixed and ignited. Gases are created which expand under pressure to move a piston in the chamber. The piston, in turn, drives a crankshaft or rotors to cause movement, e.g. in car wheels and aeroplane propellors.

HISTORY

PAPER I

1. ◆ William stripped the English nobles of their lands and privileges.
   ◆ Anybody who rebelled was dealt with harshly, for example when the North rebelled in 1069–70. William used the scorched earth policy to ensure future rebels would understand the consequences of such attacks.
   ◆ The governmental system of law was changed so that the king was the principle authority figure.
   ◆ Anglo-Saxon customs of 300 years were replaced by a new culture and French dialect was introduced.
   ◆ The feudal system was introduced in which William took the traditional Anglo-Saxon land and gave it to his Norman followers.
   ◆ He built castles all over England from where local insurrections could be dealt with.
   ◆ He commissioned the Domesday Book.

2. ◆ In 1205 King John quarrelled with the Pope Innocent III about who should be archbishop of Canterbury. The Pope wanted a man named Stephen Langton to be archbishop, but John swore he should never come to England.
   ◆ In 1209 the pope excommunicated John and banned all services in parish churches.
   ◆ In 1212 John imposed taxes on the Barons in his attempts to regain the lost lands of Aquitaine, Poitou and Anjou.
   ◆ The Barons and Stephen Langton decided to curb the King and make him govern by the old English laws that had prevailed before the Normans.
   ◆ The Barons took up arms against King John capturing London in May 1215.
   ◆ In June the Barons took King John by surprise at Windsor and he agreed to a meeting at Runnymede.
   ◆ King John signed and sealed the document on 10 June, 1215.
   ◆ The royal chancery produced a formal royal grant, based on the agreements reached at Runnymede, which became known as Magna Carta.

- The most important provisions of the Magna Carta were: that the Church was to be free from royal interference, especially in the election of bishops; that no taxes except the regular feudal dues were to be levied, except by the consent of the Great Council, or Parliament; the right to due process which led to Trial by Jury; that all weights and measures were to be kept uniform.

3. **Causes:**
   - After the Black Death, many lords gave the peasants on their estates their freedom and paid them to work on their land. Thirty-five years later, peasants feared the lords would take back these privileges.
   - Peasants wanted to be free of the burden of working unpaid on Church land and were supported by a priest from Kent called John Ball.
   - The long war with France had cost money, which mostly came from the peasants through taxes. In 1380, Richard II introduced the Poll Tax. By 1381, the peasants had had enough.
   - In May 1381, a tax collector investigating the Essex village of Fobbing was thrown out by the villagers. In June, soldiers arrived and were also thrown out. The villagers then marched on London to plead with the young King.

Course:
- Wat Tyler from Kent emerged as the leader of the peasants. As they marched to London, they had destroyed tax records and tax registers. Buildings which housed government records were burnt.
- By mid-June many peasants were drunk in London, looting took place and foreigners were murdered. Wat Tyler had asked for discipline but he did not get it.
- On 14 June, the King met the rebels at Mile End giving the peasants all that they demanded and asking that they return home. Some did but others murdered the archbishop and Treasurer. Richard II spent the night in hiding.
- On 15 June, he met the rebels again at Smithfield outside of the city's walls. At this meeting, the Lord Mayor killed Wat Tyler. His death and Richard's promise to give the

peasants what they asked for was enough to send them home.

Results:

- By the summer of 1381, the revolt was over. John Ball was hanged. Richard did not keep any of his promises, claiming that they were made under threat and were therefore not valid in law. Other leaders from both Kent and Essex were hanged.
- The Poll Tax was withdrawn but the peasants were forced back into their old way of life – under the control of the lord of the manor.
- The Black Death had caused a shortage of labour and over the next 100 years many peasants asked for more money and the lords had to give it.

4.
- Initially Warwick had been a supporter of King Edward IV; together they had put down Lancastrian rebels.
- Warwick became very powerful when he inherited the earldom of Salisbury in 1462, thus having two earldoms.
- By the late 1460s the relationship between the King and Warwick had broken down and Warwick had formed an alliance with Edward's brother Clarence.
- Together they defeated Edward's forces at the Battle of Edgecote, capturing the King amongst others. He ruled briefly, but then realized he couldn't rule with the King imprisoned. Thus the King was released and gradually reasserted political control.
- After another rebellion in 1470, Warwick fled to France attained as a traitor. Whilst there he formed an alliance with his old enemy Margaret of Anjou, exiled queen of King Henry VI – who had been deposed by Edward in 1461.
- He led an army into England and deposed Edward IV into exile, while Henry VI was made king.
- Warwick now planned to consolidate his alliance with King Louis XI by helping France to invade Burgundy, for which King Louis promised him the reward of the Burgundian territories of Zeeland and Holland. News of this drove Charles the Bold, Duke of Burgundy, to assist Edward with funds and an army to invade England in the spring of 1471. By the time Margaret and her supporters

were ready to join Warwick from France, Warwick had been defeated and killed by the returning Edward IV at the Battle of Barnet.

5. ♦ Establishment of Royal Magistrates Courts, which allowed officials to adjudicate on dispute with authority to the crown, thus reducing the workload on the Royal Courts and allowing justice to be delivered with better efficiency.
    ♦ Improvements in the legal system, with trial by jury becoming the standard procedure for cases.
    ♦ The Constitutions of Clarendon, a set of legislative procedures that decreased ecclesiastical interference from Rome.

6. ♦ Many in Brittany believed that John was responsible for the murder of his nephew, Arthur, in 1202.
    ♦ In 1204, John's army was defeated in Brittany. His military standing fell and he was nicknamed John Softsword. To pay for the defeat, John increased taxes.
    ♦ In 1207 John quarrelled with the pope over who should be Archbishop of Canterbury. He was excommunicated and England was put under a law that stated that no christening or marriage would be legal.
    ♦ In 1213, John surrendered the spiritual well-being of the country to the pope, who proclaimed that anybody who tried to overthrow John would be legally entitled to do so.
    ♦ In the same year, John lost a battle to the French at Bouvines and England lost all her possessions in France. The Barons rebelled in 1214.

7. ♦ A village would normally have three large fields throughout which each farmer's land was distributed in scattered strips separated by balks, with another area set aside for common grazing.
    ♦ Farming was coordinated by the landowner's steward or reeve. Two fields would be cultivated (usually with corn) each year, the third being left fallow.

8. ♦ Edward expanded the administration into four principal parts: the Chancery, the Exchequer, the Household, and the Council.
    ♦ Royal jurisdiction became supreme: the Exchequer developed a court to hear financial disputes, the Court of

Common Pleas arose to hear property disputes, and the Court of the King's Bench addressed criminal cases in which the king had a vested interest.

♦ A major campaign to control Llywelyn ap Gruffydd of Wales began in 1277 and lasted until Llywelyn's death in 1282. Wales was divided into shires, English civil law was introduced, and the region was administered by appointed justices.

♦ Edward constructed many new castles to ensure his conquest. In 1301, the king's eldest son was named Prince of Wales, a title still granted.

♦ He retained English holdings in France through diplomacy, but was drawn into war by the incursions of Philip IV in Gascony. He negotiated peace with France in 1303 and retained those areas England held before the war.

♦ He finally subjugated Scotland after many battles.

♦ Parliament reaffirmed Magna Carta and the Charter of the Forest; it was concluded that no tax should be levied without consent of the realm as a whole (as represented by Parliament).

9. ♦ Henry honoured his pledge of December 1483 to marry Elizabeth of York, daughter and heir of King Edward IV. The marriage unified the warring houses.

♦ Henry had the Titulus Regius, the document that declared Edward IV's children illegitimate by citing his marriage as invalid, repealed in his first parliament, thus legitimizing his wife.

♦ He introduced ruthless mechanisms of taxation.

♦ He introduced the King's Council that kept the nobility in check.

♦ He concluded the Treaty of Medina Del Campo in 1489, by which his son, Arthur Tudor, was married to Catherine of Aragon and a treaty between England and Scotland that betrothed his daughter Margaret to King James IV of Scotland, a move which would ultimately see the English and Scottish crowns united under James I. He formed an alliance with the Holy Roman Empire, under the Emperor Maximilian I (1493–1519) and persuaded Pope Innocent VIII to issue a Bull of Excommunication against all pretenders to his throne.

10. ◆ Initially a committed Catholic, Henry was awarded the title 'Defender of the Faith' after countering Luther's attack on the Church during the Protestant Reformation in Saxony from 1517 onwards.

   ◆ This changed when Henry made the decision to extricate himself from a marriage that had produced no male heir.

   ◆ In 1527 Henry asked Pope Clement VII to annul the marriage, but the Pope refused. Henry's desire for Anne Boleyn increased.

   ◆ His Chancellor, Cardinal Wolsey, was unable to secure the annulment and was charged with praemunire.

   ◆ The Parliament summoned in 1529 to deal with annulment became known as the Reformation Parliament.

   ◆ Thomas Cromwell saw how the English Parliament could be used to advance Royal supremacy, and as it seemed that the Pope would not change his mind, with Charles V having just sacked Rome in 1527 other alternatives started to form in his mind about how Henry could secure his divorce.

   ◆ In October 1530 a meeting of clergy and lawyers advised that Parliament could not empower the archbishop to act against the Pope's prohibition. Henry resolved to charge the whole English clergy with praemunire in order to secure their agreement to his annulment. Henry claimed £100,000 from the Convocation of Canterbury of the Church of England for their pardon, which was granted on 24 January 1531. The clergy wanted the payment to be spread over five years; Henry refused. The Convocation withdrew their payment and demanded Henry fulfil certain guarantees. Henry refused and ordered that the clergy recognize him as the 'sole protector and Supreme Head of the Church and clergy of England'; that the King had spiritual jurisdiction; that the privileges of the Church were upheld only if they did not detract from the royal prerogative and the laws of the realm; that the King pardoned the clergy for violating the statute of praemunire; and that the laity were also pardoned.

   ◆ Bishop John Fisher inserted into the first article the phrase 'as far as the word of God allows'. In Convocation, Archbishop Warham requested a discussion but when met by silence said: 'He who is silent seems to consent' to which a clergyman present responded: 'Then we are all silent.' The Convocation granted consent to the King's five articles and the payment on 8 March 1531. That same year Parliament passed the Act of Pardon.

- In 1532, Cromwell brought before Parliament the Supplication Against the Ordinaries which listed nine grievances against the Church.
- On 10 May, the King demanded of Convocation that the Church should renounce all authority to make laws and, on 15 May, the Submission of the Clergy was subscribed, which recognized Royal Supremacy over the Church. The day after this More resigned as Chancellor, leaving Cromwell as Henry's chief minister.
- Thereafter there followed a series of Acts of Parliament, for example The Act in Conditional Restraint of Annates which proposed that the clergy should pay no more than 5% of their first year's revenue (annates) to Rome.
- The Act in Restraint of Appeals which was drafted by Cromwell declared England an independent country in every respect.
- The Act in Absolute Restraint of Annates outlawed all annates to Rome, and also ordered that if cathedrals refused the King's nomination for bishop, they would be liable to punishment by praemunire.
- In 1534 the Act of Supremacy made Henry 'supreme head on earth of the Church of England' and disregarded any 'usage, custom, foreign laws, foreign authority [or] prescription'.
- The King moved to take control over much of the Church's property through the dissolution of the monasteries.

11. • Before Elizabeth took the throne England and Spain had been united because of the marriage of Mary I and Phillip II of Spain.
- After Mary's death Phillip had wanted to marry Elizabeth. She refused.
- Internally Elizabeth was threatened by a Catholic uprising in the North in 1569, thus her initial policy of following a Middle Path in religion hardened.
- The English looted many ships they found on the High Seas and Elizabeth, rather than punishing them was

quite happy to receive their stolen, often Spanish, booty. An attack in 1568 by Spain on English privateers, illegally trading in the West Indies increased tensions.

- At about the same time, four Spanish ships took refuge from pirates in England. Elizabeth detained them and seized the bullion.
- During the 1570s, Elizabeth lent small sums of money to the rebels and allowed English volunteers to go to their aid.
- In 1575, the Spanish government went bankrupt, and its unpaid troops went on a rampage. This temporarily united every important interest in the Netherlands against Spain. But when Calvinist enthusiasts in Ghent and other large cities began to impose their beliefs on the Catholic population, the Netherlands split in two, with the southern provinces forming the Union of Arras, and making peace with Spain, and the northern provinces repudiating Philip's rule.
- Spain made a renewed effort to reconquer the whole area and Elizabeth finally decided that she must commit troops to prevent Dutch collapse. In December, Robert Dudley Earl of Leicester arrived with a force of about 7,000 men but saw little success.
- Privateering continued and was used as a proxy navy, though Elizabeth was also building up a state navy. From about 1586, Philip II began building a large navy of his own with which to attack England.
- Elizabeth ordered Sir Francis Drake to launch a pre-emptive strike against Philip. He sailed into the harbour of Cadiz and destroyed about 10,000 tons of Spanish shipping.
- In 1587 Mary Queen of Scots was executed for her part in a plot to bring Catholicism back to England. Philip II, a devout Catholic, used this as an excuse to invade England.
- After the failure of the Spanish Armada Philip II continued to threaten England by building ships and sending support to Irish rebels in 1601.
- England responded by continuing to attack places like Cadiz (1598) and aiding Dutch rebels against Philips's French allies. By 1602 there were 8,000 troops fighting in the Netherlands.

12. ✦ Elizabeth faced the most serious challenge from extremists, both Catholics and Protestants.
    ✦ The Act of Supremacy made Elizabeth Supreme Governor of the Church and church officials were required to take an oath of obedience.
    ✦ The heresy laws passed in the reign of Mary were repealed and the celebration of Communion in both kinds was confirmed. Catholic bishops in the Lords were hostile to this. Two Catholic bishops were imprisoned during the Easter Recess of 1559.
    ✦ The Act of Uniformity (1559) just about passed the Lords. The 1552 Prayer Book was to be used in services while the wording of the 1549 Prayer Book was to be incorporated into the Communion service.
    ✦ To solidify her religious settlement in 1563 a set of radical articles were published which aimed to remove all superstition from the Church.

13. ✦ Laws were passed to make churches more plain. Under Edward, stained-glass windows and pictures were removed and furniture became very basic.
    ✦ Services became more plain and the common person could now understand what was being said as services – now called Holy Communion – were in English. Archbishop Cranmer wrote an English prayer book. Priests did not dress in the bright clothing associated with the Catholic Church and were allowed to marry. The king remained head of the Church.

14. ✦ Numbers of beggars and vagrants in Elizabethan England were rising.
    ✦ More people fell into poverty because of the closure of the monasteries during Henry VIII's time, the fact that retained armies were no longer allowed, the decline in the wool trade, enclosure of arable farm land, and due to a series of poor harvests in the 1590s. This law attempted to deal with the problem.
    ✦ Its provisions were that the impotent poor were to be cared for in an almshouse or a poorhouse. It offered relief to people who were unable to work, while the able-bodied poor were set to work in a House of Industry. The idle poor and vagrants were sent to a House of Correction or

even prison. Pauper children would become apprentices.

15. ♦ About a third of the population lived in poverty, increased
    after bad harvests. A shortage of food resulted in higher
    prices.
    ♦ Wealthy people were expected to give alms to the poor.
    Some were generous while others were not, meaning that
    the poor in some villages were well cared for while others
    starved.
    ♦ When large landowners changed from arable to sheep
    farming, unemployment increased rapidly. The closing of
    the monasteries created more unemployment.
    ♦ The unemployed were often tempted to leave their villages
    to look for work. This was illegal and people who did this
    were classified as vagabonds.
    ♦ Retained armies were no longer allowed, creating many
    unemployed soldiers.

16. ♦ British ships were sent around the world to search for
    new trading partners and to establish trading routes. In
    the process new lands were discovered and mapped.
    ♦ John Cabot was employed by the British government
    to discover new lands from 1497 onwards and went to
    Newfoundland and Nova Scotia. Various companies like
    the Muscovy Company, Levant Company and the
    Hudson's Bay Company and later the Honourable East
    India Company were set up to enable trade and English
    bases were set up in the Baltic in the 1570s in Hanse
    ports.
    ♦ In 1578, Sir Francis Drake, in the course of his
    circumnavigation of the world, discovered Cape Horn at
    the tip of South America. The sea between this and
    Antarctica is now known as Drake Passage.
    ♦ Richard Hakluyt, an English writer, is remembered for
    his efforts in promoting and supporting the settlement of
    North America by the English through his works.
    ♦ Apart from voyages of exploration and trading, privateers
    were also common and Elizabeth did little to discourage
    them.
    ♦ The failed Spanish Armada reflects the might and
    ingenuity of English sea captains like Drake and Raleigh.
    ♦ England's geography as an island kingdom also

encouraged sailors in an age when sea voyages were common and it was but another way of showing the country's greatness.

17. ◆ James's reaction to the Monmouth rebellion was to plan the increase of the standing army and the appointment of loyal and experienced Roman Catholic officers.
   ◆ This, together with James's attempts to give civic equality to Roman Catholic and Protestant dissenters, led to conflict with Parliament, as it was seen as James showing favouritism towards Roman Catholics.
   ◆ James prorogued Parliament in 1685 and ruled without it.
   ◆ He attempted to promote the Roman Catholic cause by dismissing judges and Lord Lieutenants who refused to support the withdrawal of laws penalizing religious dissidents. Within three years, the majority of James's subjects had been alienated.
   ◆ In 1687 James issued the Declaration of Indulgence aimed at religious toleration; seven bishops who asked James to reconsider were charged with seditious libel, but later acquitted to popular Anglican acclaim.
   ◆ His second (Roman Catholic) wife, Mary of Modena, gave birth on 10 June 1688 to a son and it seemed that a Roman Catholic dynasty would be established.
   ◆ William of Orange, Protestant husband of James's elder daughter Mary, invaded on 5 November 1688.
   ◆ The Army and the Navy deserted to William, and James fled to France.
   ◆ James's attempt to regain the throne by taking a French army to Ireland failed – he was defeated at the Battle of the Boyne in 1690.

18. ◆ William III of England had promised to support the Emperor's (Leopold I) claim to the undivided Spanish Succession.
   ◆ Two partition treaties were signed to split the succession territories, however the French were unhappy with the result. Thus Louis XIV cut off the English and the Dutch from Spanish trade, threatening the commercial interests of both.
   ◆ William III secured the support of his subjects and negotiated the Treaty of Den Haag with the United

Provinces and Austria. The agreement, reached on
7 September 1701, recognized Philip V as King of Spain,
but allotted Austria the Spanish territories in Italy,
forcing it to accept as well the Spanish Netherlands, thus
protecting that crucial region from French control.
England and the Netherlands, meanwhile, were to retain
their commercial rights in Spain.

- A few days after the signing of the treaty, the former King
  of England, James II (who had been deposed by William
  III in 1688) died in France. Although Louis had treated
  William as King of England since the Treaty of Ryswick,
  he now recognized James II's son, James Francis Edward
  Stuart, as the rightful monarch. Louis's action alienated
  the English public even further, and gave William
  grounds for war.

- From the Treaty of Utrecht, France ceded to Britain's
  claims to the Hudson Bay Company territories in Rupert's
  Land, Newfoundland and Acadia. St Kitts was also ceded
  to Britain. France was required to recognize British
  suzerainty over the Iroquois and commerce with the Far
  Indians was to be open to traders of all nations.

19. • James lacked the fiscal abilities to govern without conflict
      from Parliament. He sold Crown lands, despite being
      urged to let the Privy Council run them, and sold
      government offices and positions, devaluing the work of
      other officials. He also promoted his friends.

    • In 1604 James prorogued Parliament after failing to win
      its support for a full union of the crowns or financial union.

    • In February 1610 a believer in parliamentary
      participation in government (Robert Cecil) proposed a
      scheme, known as the Great Contract, whereby
      Parliament, in return for ten royal concessions, would
      grant a lump sum of £600,000 to pay off the king's debts
      plus an annual grant of £200,000.

    • James lost patience with negotiations and dismissed
      Parliament on 31 December 1610.

    • The same pattern was repeated with the so-called 'Addled
      Parliament' of 1614, which James dissolved after a mere
      eight weeks when Commons hesitated to grant him the
      money he required.

- James ruled without Parliament until 1621, employing officials such as the businessman Lionel Cranfield.
- In November 1621, led by Sir Edward Coke, Parliament framed a petition asking not only for war with Spain but also for Prince Charles to marry a Protestant, and for enforcement of the anti-Catholic laws.
- They issued a statement protesting their rights, including freedom of speech. James ripped the protest out of the record book and dissolved Parliament again.
- A war against the Spanish made James call another Parliament in 1623 to ask for funds. The outcome of the Parliament of 1624 was ambiguous: James still refused to declare war, but Prince Charles believed the Commons had committed themselves to financing a war against Spain.

20. - A new Act of Uniformity was passed that made Puritan acts of worship illegal. Those that refused to obey this law became known as non-conformists or dissenters. Large numbers of non-conformists went to prison.
- Men who had been Anglicans before the Civil War were appointed to senior posts in the Church. Bishops once again became members of the House of Lords.
- Puritans lost their power in politics, were excluded from universities and from teaching. Strict censorship was also imposed on books.
- In 1670 Charles became a Roman Catholic. However, as Parliament and about 90 per cent of the people in England were Protestants, Charles kept this a secret. He tried to protect other Catholics from Protestant persecution but was unable to stop Parliament from passing the Test Acts that prevented Catholics from being Members of Parliament.
- In Ireland the church was re-established.

21. - Walpole negotiated a treaty with France and Prussia in 1725.
- He uncovered Jacobite threats and protected George I from attacks.
- Under George II he is seen as the first real Prime Minister and 10 Downing Street became his residence.
- Because he followed a policy of avoiding war he was able to lower taxes.

- He managed to secure the position of the Hanoverian dynasty and countervailed Jacobitism.

22.
- The Tories had been discredited after the Jacobite Uprising of 1715. Many were seen as traitorous.
- The Septennial Act of 1715 increased the maximum length of Parliament from three to seven years, thus keeping the Whigs in power for longer. They won the 1715 and 1722 elections.

23.
- James attempted to relax the penal laws and supported a policy of religious toleration. By allying himself with the Catholics, dissenters and nonconformists he hoped to build a coalition that would advance Catholic emancipation.
- In 1686, James coerced the Court of the King's Bench into deciding that the King could dispense with religious restrictions of the Test Acts. He ordered the removal of the anti-Catholic Bishop of London and dismissed Protestant fellows of Magdalen College, Oxford.
- He created a large standing army, employing Catholics in positions of power. He also prorogued Parliament without its consent.
- The army in Ireland was purged of Protestants.
- In April 1688, James reissued the Declaration of Indulgence and ordered all clergymen to read it in their churches. When the Archbishop of Canterbury, William Sancroft, and six other bishops wrote to James asking him to reconsider his policies, they were arrested on charges of seditious libel.
- James fathered a son. Until then his crown would have passed to his first daughter, Mary, a Protestant. This was too much for Parliament who wanted to put Mary and her husband, William – a stadholder of the main provinces of the Dutch Republic – on the throne.

24.
- Colonization began in the late sixteenth century and was established under a system of Proprietary Governments, who were appointed under mercantile charters to English joint stock companies to found and run settlements.
- In 1664, England took over the Province of New York and Delaware and in 1714 Britain acquired the French colony of Acadia.

- With varying degrees of success, multiple trading companies were set up to support the new colonies and trade goods with Britain.

25.
- The Navigation Acts protected English shipping, and secured a profit to the home country from the colonies.
- There were cultural and political clashes in culture between the American colonists and their English rulers.
- In 1763 the Treaty of Paris was signed ending the French and Indian Wars and thus removing a threat to the colonies. At the same time the British taxed sugar and molasses in 1764 more keenly and were more prepared to enforce the collection of this tax.
- The Stamp Act of 1765 demanded direct revenue back to Britain. Many complained and societies called the Sons of Liberty were formed to protest, campaigning for no taxation without representation.
- The Stamp Act was repealed but the government passed an act declaring its rights to tax the colonies.
- The Townsend Acts were designed to collect revenue from the colonists in America by putting customs duties on imports of glass, lead, paints, paper and tea. The colonials, spurred on by the writings of John Dickinson, Samuel Adams and others, protested against the taxes.
- Five men were killed in the Boston Massacre of 1770.
- The Townsend Acts were repealed, but the tax on tea was kept. A monopoly was granted to the East India Company and this led to the Boston Tea Party.
- Parliament then passed the 'Intolerable Acts' (which limited the political and geographical freedom of the colonists) and this led to the Continental Congress of 1774 to build colonial unity.
- Before the Congress could meet again the war had begun in Lexington.

26.
- The end of the Napoleonic Wars led to famine and unemployment. There was a depression in textile manufacture and weavers and spinners saw their wages decrease. The Corn Law exacerbated the problem by imposing a tax on imports: people were forced to buy more expensive and poorer quality British grain. There were riots in London and elsewhere in protest.

* Petitions were sent to government demanding free trade.
* There was a desire for political reform, especially in Lancashire. A lack of suffrage for many in the North of England resulted in the infamous Peterloo Massacre in 1819 at which people were protesting about the Corn Laws and lack of suffrage.

27. * Naval battles at Trafalgar
    * Peninsular Wars. The British Army under Wellington helped the Portuguese to fight against the France in Portugal and construct the Lines of Torres Vedras, which repelled the French Army. Wellington used a scorched earth policy thus the French were not able to live on the land. This was the beginning of the need for the French troops in the Iberian Peninsula.

28. * Determined to recover the prerogative lost to the ministerial council by the first two Georges, he weakened the Whig party through bribery, coercion and patronage.
    * Prime Minister, William Pitt the Elder was toppled by Whigs after the Peace of Paris (1783), and men of mediocre talent and servile minds were hand-picked by George as Cabinet members, acting as little more than yes-men.

29. * At the time of George III's accession, cottage industries had sprung up whereby production of products like textiles were done in-house. Although enclosure had started it was not endemic as it would become by the mid-nineteenth century. In the middle of the nineteenth century there was greater movement between villages with vast transport improvements. Since life expectancy had also increased, where a person was born was often not where they would die.

30. * Towards the end of the eighteenth century, Scottish economist Adam Smith argued in *The Wealth of Nations* (1776) that trade works best when it is free from government interference, and the notion became important to Victorian industrialists.
    * In 1815, Parliament passed the Corn Laws, which placed high tariffs on foreign corn, meaning that it was costly to import. The aim of the laws was to protect British farmers

from being undersold, but in actual fact they led to bread shortages and hunger.

* In the late 1830s, the Anti-Corn Law League, including John Bright and Richard Cobden, campaigned against the laws, until they were repealed by Prime Minister Robert Peel in 1846.
* As Chancellor, Liberalist MP William Gladstone pushed to promote free trade, working to reduce public expenditures and completing free trade budgets.
* The British pursued a policy of low import and export tariffs in order to encourage free trade.

31. * Initially the American Patriots had more support and controlled more colonies. After the British issued the Proclamation of Rebellion there was to be no negotiation with the 'traitors' despite the Olive Branch petition.
* Only about a quarter to a third of colonists remained loyal to the British government.
* Following the Battle of Bunker Hill in June 1776 the Patriots had control of all the territory and population, leaving the Loyalists powerless, existing state governments had been overthrown and British agents and governors were evicted from their homes.
* On 4 July 1776 the Declaration of Independence was adopted followed by the Articles of Confederation which united the states against the British.
* Actions of key individuals like George Washington, James Madison, John Adams, Benjamin Franklin and Thomas Jefferson were also important.
* The British returned in force in August 1776 and had some victories, but ultimately lost because of a surprise attack by Washington.
* The French, and later Spain and the Dutch, also decided to enter the war. The British were fighting on several fronts, and the stalemate in the northern theatre of war forced them to try to make a breakthrough in the south.
* The British were defeated there since there were not enough Loyalists to fight with them. Against a combined US French assault the British had to surrender.
* George III wanted to fight on but his supporters lost control in Parliament and the war ended.

32. ◆ Before the reign of George III Turnpike Trusts had been set up to build and take tolls from the users of main roads. This developed under the reign of George III.

    ◆ Completed in 1776 the Bridgewater Canal was the catalyst for half a century of canal building. James Brindley was the leading canal engineer of his time and built the 'Grand Cross' of canals which linked the four great river basins of Britain. In 1793 an Act was passed to authorize the Grand Junction Canal from Braunston on the Oxford Canal, to Brentford on the River Thames west of London. London was not joined directly to the national canal network until 1801 with the opening of the Paddington Arm of the Grand Junction Canal.

    ◆ In 1782 James Watt invented the first steam engine able to turn wheels. In 1789 William Jessop used flanged iron wheels on iron edge rails on a coal railway at Loughborough. In 1794 the Peak Forest Tramway opened with the first non-mine narrow gauge railway. In 1802 the Carmarthenshire Tramroad, later the Llanelly and Mynydd Mawr Railway, located in south-west Wales, was established by Act of Parliament. In 1803 the first public railway, the Surrey Iron Railway opened in south London. In 1807 the first fare-paying, passenger railway service in the world was established on the Oystermouth Railway in Swansea, Wales. In 1814 George Stephenson constructed his first locomotive, *Blücher*.

33. ◆ The Reform Act of 1867 extended the franchise by nearly one million men thus granting them representation in the House of Commons. Disraeli introduced many Acts with his Conservative government to improve social conditions in Great Britain, including the Artisan's and Labourers' Dwellings Improvement Act (1875), the Public Health Act (1875), the Sale of Food and Drugs Act (1875) and the Education Act (1876). His government also introduced a new Factory Act meant to protect workers, the Conspiracy and Protection of Property Act (1875) to allow peaceful picketing, and the Employers and Workmen Act (1875) to enable workers to sue employers in the civil courts if they broke legal contracts.

34. ◆ In the short term Britain went to war to defend Belgium's

neutrality. However there were more long-term and complicated reasons to support this thesis.

- ◆ Germany's foreign policy in the build-up to WWI had been aggressive, both in Morocco with the French and in South Africa with the strange Krüger Telegram incident.
- ◆ There was also an Arms race operating in Europe at the time. In particular Britain and Germany were competing to build up their navies.
- ◆ Britain was concerned to keep its military and colonial reputation intact and was allied to both France and Russia. However these were more treaties of friendship and did not constitute a deal to defend either country if attacked.

35. (a) John Stuart Mill's book *Principles of Political Economy* (1871) argued that the working classes, in joining together, could secure better wages and better condition. It wasn't until the emergence of the New Unions in the late 1880s that progress was made. Unions also played a role in the creation of the Labour Representation Committee that effectively formed the basis for the Labour Party. Between 1910 and 1914 there was industrial unrest and a massive increase in trade union membership.

(b) WWI saw an enormous increase in union membership and widespread recognition of unions and their increased involvement in management.

36. ◆ Provisions included: free school meals (1906), the introduction of schools to provide medical care and checks for children (1907), the Old Age Pension Act (1908), the ban of back-to-back housing and enforcement of building regulations (1909), and the introduction of National Health Insurance for workers (1911).

37. ◆ In May 1894 he joined the Independent Labour Party, becoming Secretary of the Labour Representation Committee. In cooperation with the Liberals, Labour was allowed to contest a number of working-class seats, which gave the ILP its first breakthrough into the House of Commons.
- ◆ In 1906 he was elected MP for Leicester for the new Labour Party.

- In 1911 he became leader of the Labour Party. He did not support the war, thus resigned as leader in 1914 and became Treasurer.
- After losing his seat in 1918, he regained it in 1922 after the Conservatives left the Liberal Conservative coalition. Liberals were losing power and Labour became the main opposition party, making him Leader of the Opposition.
- He was the first Labour Prime Minister in 1924 and took the post of Foreign Minister, wanting to undo the damage of the Treaty of Versailles.
- His second period as PM came during the crisis of depression where he formed a National Government in which many of the MPs were Conservative. Thus he was expelled from the Labour Party

38. - People had to cope with tremendous loss of life. Those who had fought became known as the Lost Generation and many returning soldiers suffered from post-traumatic stress and shellshock.
    - Huge war debts meant Britain had little money for import payments, so people were deprived of produce from abroad and forced to pay higher prices for food.
    - Unemployment levels increased, with many wounded soldiers unfit to work, and the infrastructure of industries damaged or destroyed.
    - The government had difficulties coping with the housing demands after buildings had been destroyed: homelessness increased.

39. - Local agriculture unions were being formed all over Britain in the 1870s in a bid to combat low wages received and poor working conditions.
    - A series of wet summers damaged grain crops. Cattle farmers were hit by foot-and-mouth disease, and sheep farmers by sheep liver rot. The poor harvests, however, worsened the threat to British agriculture from growing imports of foodstuffs from abroad. The development of the steamship and the establishment of a railroad network in the USA, together with the invention of the refrigeration car, allowed US farmers to export hard grain to Britain at a price that undercut the British farmer. At the same time, large amounts of cheap corned beef started to arrive

from Argentina, and the creation of the Suez Canal opened the British market to cheap lamb and wool from Australia and New Zealand. By 1900, half of the meat eaten in Britain came from abroad.

- There was a shift to higher-cost, high-quality produce such as fruit and vegetables, and high-quality meat. Farmers took land out of production and cut employment (400,000 jobs were lost in farming between 1870 and 1900). To aid agricultural labourers Joseph Arch formed the National Agricultural Labourers' Union in 1872 (the first of its kind), although it collapsed in 1896 after opposition from farmers.
- The government set up the Board of Agriculture in 1889, to offer advice. Two Smallholdings Acts were also passed (1893 and 1907) to allow farm workers to buy small farms.

40.
- The rearmament of Germany broke the Treaty of Versailles.
- Hitler's allies increased in aggression (Italy and Japan).
- The Treaty of St Germain was broken by the Anschluss of Germany with Austria (March 1938) and the annexation of the Sudetenland.
- The Nazis occupied Czechoslovakia in March 1939.
- The Nazi–Soviet pact followed by the invasion of Poland (1 September 1939) finally forced Britain to war.

PAPER II

1.
- Britain desired to defend financial interests of chartered companies founded earlier, like the British South Africa Company or the East India Company.
- The Industrial Revolution motivated the search for new markets especially after the depression of 1875.
- The emergence of new powers that challenged British dominance also spurred it back into colonizing frenzy, like the newly unified Germany. Britain wished to maintain dominance in the world and felt insecure in its position.

2.
- New dominant industrial economies emerged. After Germany unified in 1871 it was a massive industrial powerhouse with access to central European markets and new resources.
- New industrial techniques also contributed, for example

German steel production increased more than tenfold. Britain struggled to compete.

* The development of chemicals and the use of electricity also helped challenged Britain's industrial supremacy.
* The use of artificial fertilizers increased agriculture yields and led to the cheaper production of dyes and alkalis.

3. ◆ In 1904 Britain established the Entente Cordiale with France and three years later the Triple Entente with Russia. Germany was perceived as a threat, with their naval presence increasing in the North Sea, so the British asked the French to move their ships in order to protect the Mediterranean and the English Channel while some of the British fleet was relocated to the North Sea.

◆ As Britain felt threatened by Germany's Weltpolitik policy, its foreign policy moved closer to Europe than the colonies. After Germany had refused to make an alliance with Britain, the British had no choice but to try to move closer to its former enemies, or risk isolation.

4. (a) A commercial arrangement in which preferential rates for trade were granted between members of the British Empire (and later of the British Commonwealth). It was a form of protectionism that promoted the unity and affluence of member nations.

(b) Imperial preference was advocated by colonial secretary Joseph Chamberlain at the end of the nineteenth century. He believed that Britain needed to cooperate with her colonies to avoid economic disaster.

However, with free trade ideas being promoted by leading economists, several Conservative MPs, including Chancellor of the Exchequer C. T. Ritchie, stood opposed. This changed in 1924 when Baldwin, a strong supporter of imperial preference, became Prime Minister and, in 1926, the Empire Marketing Board was established to encourage the British to buy from trade partners.

In 1932, trade agreements were negotiated between Britain, the Dominions and the Colonies in Canada. Known as the Ottawa Agreements, they lowered tariffs on British goods and increased duties on Dominion produce.

5. ◆ In 1904 the British formed the Entente Cordiale with France and in 1907 the Triple Entente with Russia, in order to stave off any potential threat from German naval presence.
   ◆ Britain was also involved in the Boer War from 1899–1902, a successful attempt to retain territory in South Africa.
   ◆ Britain sought to ally itself with Europe, rather than the colonies, in order to avoid isolation when faced with the perceived threat of German's policy of Weltpolitik.

6. ◆ The canal allowed for two-way water transportation of goods and people between Europe and Africa.
   ◆ It gave the British a far quicker route to their Asian possessions. Although the canal was open to all vessels, without discrimination in war or peace, the British considered the canal vital to the maintenance of their maritime and colonial interests. The British were able to penetrate Africa far more easily.

7. ◆ After World War I, Indians were demanding independence and representation in the running of their country.
   ◆ The Rowlatt Act (1919) was passed followed by a massacre at Amritsar.
   ◆ The introduction of Salt Tax prompted Gandhi to lead his people in protest.
   ◆ The Congress Party accused the British government of being sympathetic to fascism. The party was furious when the Viceroy of India declared war on Germany: it was clear that the British believed that India was subservient to the British government.

8. ◆ Germany invaded Poland. Great Britain wanted to act against Nazi expansionism since it was clear that the policy of appeasement had failed. Direct action against the aggressive nation was now necessary to preserve the security of Britain.

9. The main problems included:
   ◆ Apportioning of blame for the war
   ◆ How to go about the necessary reparations
   ◆ Territorial problems, and deciding which countries should benefit from Germany's defeat
   ◆ Granting Poland access to the sea

- ◆ How to curb German's aggression, especially concerning France who had been invaded twice in living history

10. ◆ This was the charter of the League of Nations that set out how the League was going to be run.
- ◆ The Secretariat was to be responsible for the administration of League policies and programmes and was to be housed in Geneva, Switzerland.
- ◆ The Council was to be composed of nine member nations. Britain, France, Italy, Japan and the United States were to be permanent Council members. The remaining four positions were to be chosen by the Assembly on a rotating basis.
- ◆ All member nations were to be represented in the Assembly and each was to have a single vote.
- ◆ League members pledged to: protect the territorial integrity of other member states (Article X); submit to the League disputes that threatened war; employ economic and military sanctions against nations that resorted to war; participate in arms reduction programmes; and assist in the establishment of a Permanent International Court of Justice.

11. ◆ In the first 100 days Roosevelt was given a range of powers in order to get America back on track.
- ◆ The Federal Government gave $500 million to the States to feed, house and clothe the people who were left destitute.
- ◆ Roosevelt closed all the banks and shut down permanently those that were not effective. He set up many of the so-called 'Alphabet Agencies' to provide work for the unemployed. He also dealt with problems in agriculture and in factories to ensure that farmers got fair prices and workers were ensured employment on a fair basis.
- ◆ He took power away from the States governments and increased the power of the Federal government.
- ◆ These powers were given to Roosevelt to ensure a centralized and organized approach to dealing with the depression.

12. ◆ The Ottoman Empire controlled the Dardenelles, thus was able to cut off supplies to Russia from the Mediterranean

Sea. This also forced Britain to divert troops that might otherwise have been used on the western front to Egypt and Mesopotamia for use against the Ottoman Empire.

- The Allies were afraid that the Ottoman Empire's entrance into the war would encourage other Islamic countries to join the fight against them.
- In March and April, Britain opened a new front when it attempted to invade the Gallipoli Peninsula of the Ottoman Empire.
- Although the operation should have succeeded, problems with the British decision-making process denied the enterprise both careful planning and the element of surprise.
- After a series of preliminary bombardments from the navy, which served little purpose except to alert the enemy, a strong British-French battle fleet, consisting of 16 battleships, entered the Dardanelles on March 18. It had virtually silenced the forts when some of the ships blundered into a minefield and three ships sank. Admiral Sir John De Robeck, the fleet commander, drew back.
- The Allies withdrew from the peninsula during December 1915 and early January 1916, and the Gallipoli Campaign ended.
- British forces continued fighting against the Ottomans, later in the Middle East. In Mesopotamia a British army under Sir Frederick Maude recaptured the city of Kut-al-Imara (Al Kut) early in 1917, pushed on to Baghdad in March, and inflicted a heavy defeat on the Ottomans at the city of Ramadi in September. In the region of Palestine, which the Ottoman Empire ruled, the British made two unsuccessful attacks in the spring of 1917 on the coastal fortress of Gaza. In November, British general Edmund Allenby outflanked and overwhelmed Gaza, and after hard fighting, captured Jerusalem in December 1917. German troops under General Falkenhayn reinforced the Ottomans, who tried to recover Jerusalem during the last week of December. However, Allenby and his troops defeated them.
- During this campaign the Arabs of the Hejaz (Al Hijāz) region of Arabia revolted against the Ottomans in an attempt to gain their independence. They were aided by Englishman T. E. Lawrence, who became known as

Lawrence of Arabia.

13. ◆ Attlee initially tried to continue the foreign policy of his predecessor, Eden, and retain the Empire, however this was not to last long.
   ◆ He ensured French control over Indo-China (though today this might not be seen as an achievement given the number of lives lost to the cause) and Dutch control in Indonesia.
   ◆ He encouraged the sharing of defence costs of British possessions with the UN.
   ◆ He was a pragmatist and had begun to understand earlier than most the extent of Britain's relative decline and diminishing status in the new conditions of superpower politics.
   ◆ He was keen to promote and receive Marshall Aid from the USA and become its junior partner in securing democracy, thus retaining its 'global' power façade.
   ◆ The Dunkirk Treaty with France of March 1947 was seen as security against any possible revival of German power.
   ◆ By late 1947 Attlee's government was helping with the creation of NATO, a signal of resolve designed to encourage further USA support for a West European bulwark against the USSR.

14. ◆ The nuclear race. The USA exploded its first bomb in 1945, and the USSR in 1949. The arms race between the Western Powers and the USSR followed.
   ◆ The question of reparations in Germany
   ◆ The giving of Marshall Aid
   ◆ Stalin's takeover of Eastern Europe
   ◆ Kennan's Long Telegram and Churchill's Fulton speech about the Iron curtain
   ◆ The Berlin Blockade
   ◆ Soviet support for newly Communist China in the United Nations
   ◆ The Korean War

15. ◆ In the 1950s there was a huge influx of workers from the Indian sub-continent who were encouraged to seek work in Lancashire.
   ◆ An increased work force allowed the mill owners to introduce a third shift or night shift to the working routine

although many workers were unhappy with these changes.
- Britain also started to import cotton cloth from India, thus profitability decreased.

16.
- Woodrow Wilson was President of America after WWI. Even though America had only got involved in 1917 it wanted to ensure that another war on such a scale would never happen again. Thus Wilson came up with the Fourteen Points upon which he wanted the Treaty of Versailles to be based. Unable to persuade Britain and France to agree to all his points, the Treaty was a compromise.
- The American public and Congress would not ratify the treaty, so the USA was unable to pass the new League of Nations.
- In WWII the USA played a leading role in ensuring that Europe did not fall to Communism. After the war at Yalta, America supplied the countries of Europe with Marshall Aid to rebuild and the USA kept troops stationed in Europe for many years. NATO was set up in 1949 to ensure peace was not threatened in Western European states.

17.
- Germany's swift defeat of the Low Countries left Churchill with hard decisions to make. He steadfastly refused to any notion of negotiating with the Germans despite other people in the Cabinet seeing it as the only option.
- He was faced with the issue of protecting Britain from imminent German attack after the inevitable fall of France.
- He had to inform the public of the progress of the war, and took political risks when he emphasized the dangers faced by Britain.
- He ensured Britain was supplied for the war, with the lend-lease scheme a product of Roosevelt and Churchill's good relationship.

18.
- Migration was an issue, with five million Hindus leaving Pakistan for India and six to seven million Muslims arriving in Pakistan.
- Acts of violence and revenge increased.
- Massacres occurred frequently, especially on the trains used by the refugees.

GEOGRAPHY

PAPER I

1. (a)

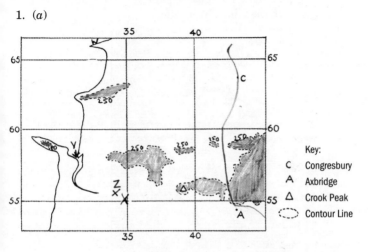

Key:
C Congresbury
A Axbridge
△ Crook Peak
⬭ Contour Line

(b) (i) Lowland X appears to be on the floodplain of the river Ax as nearby to the north the river is clearly meandering. In times of high discharge the river in the lower course is liable to flood. There are also many channels present that may be natural drainage for flood water to recede or act as drainage channels to protect fields in the region.

(ii) The absence of surface channels in the highland areas (e.g. Fry's Hill, 4355) indicate that precipitation is able to move below the surface to the underlying rock, rather than as surface runoff.

(c) (i) Compton Bishop; Bourton Farm
(ii) Winscombe Hill, Compton Hill
(iii) 414551

(d) Loxton village is situated in a col between two higher land areas (Loxton Hill to the west and Compton Hill to the east). Close to the Lox Yeo river, the location would have been ideal for access following the broad river valley whilst at he same time the river may have been a source of water for various uses. In more ancient times the location may have afforded a very good all-round view to allow for surveillance of any potential threat. On balance the access to good transport, flat and fertile alluvium for agriculture and river water would have lead to the village's situation.

2. (a)

(b) (i) The remote location makes any industrial activity difficult and the steep terrain and wet climate make arable farming systems unfavourable. Hence the abundant grassland of the region is suited to sheep farming and the employment it provides.

(ii) Coal mines attracted migrant workers from Wales and England during the period when 'Coal was King'. Low levels of mechanization meant that large numbers of miners were needed. Other industries such as metalworking agglomerated, increasing employment levels in the South Wales valleys and therefore the population density. Once these large communities became established they attracted further entrepreneurs and migration continued to fuel population growth.

3. (a) (i) A = Cambrian Mountains, B = Pennines
(ii) C = Cheshire Plains, D = Trent Valley

(*b*) and (*c*)

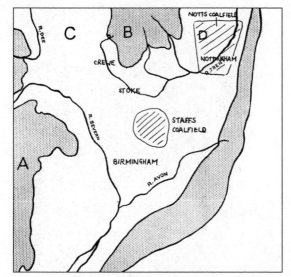

(*d*)   (i)   Often referred to as 'the backbone of England',
B contains the Peak District National Park,
as well as some of the Yorkshire Dales and
Northumberland National Park. The mountains
are a resistant Millstone grit anticline with
carboniferous limestone strata and form a
dramatic ridge with a landscape of rough grass
and low bushes. The area contains dry river
valleys, caves and potholes, which has led to
recreational uses alongside traditional pastoral
farming, utilizing traditional dry-stone walls.

    (ii)   Stoke-on-Trent is historically significant in terms
of the industrial revolution as the focus of fine china
making in the UK. Josiah Wedgwood is
synonymous with the region and the area gets its
nickname 'The Potteries' from the agglomeration of
such industries. The town owes its industrial
success to the location of the canals that aided
transportation of goods and raw materials, along
with local coal from Staffordshire and
Nottinghamshire.

4. (*a*)

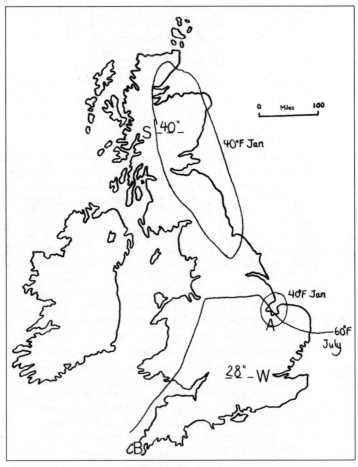

(*b*) (i) Winter temperatures at B are moderated by the influence of the North Atlantic Drift, the warm ocean current off the west of the UK. Prevailing winds from the west are warmed as they pass over this current. Further inland at A there is no such influence and thus the colder winter temperatures here give the area as a whole a much larger annual temperature change.

(ii) Prevailing winds from the west have gained moisture by evaporation from the sea, enhanced by the NAD. Thus as this air meets the Highland areas of Scotland it is forced to rise, cool and in this way large amounts of orographic rainfall occur at position S. By contrast, W can be said to be in the 'rain shadow' and not being mountainous there are not the conditions to bring on large volumes of rainfall. By the time westerly winds reach W they will have dropped a great deal of their moisture further east.

(iii) With large volumes of rainfall almost throughout the year, location B is not ideal for arable farming, with issues such as waterlogging reducing arable yields. The climate at A favours arable farming, with a balance of sunshine and rainfall and low levels of rain in the summer aiding ripening.

5. (a) *See overleaf*
   (b) (i) Manufacturing in inner London is focused in the East End Docks area, where ships bring in raw materials, break their bulk and provide a raw material location for industry. London's rivers and canal network are used to access raw materials and transport finished products.

   (ii) Manufacturing on the outskirts is focused on large-scale modern manufacturing, such as car assembly. Large areas are required for factories and road and rail transport is important for access to raw materials and distribution of products.

6. (a) Rugged upland areas – Dartmoor and the Grampian Mountains (b) Annual precipitation in the two regions is well above the UK average due to the prevailing winds and orographic effects (c) Remoteness from the main industrial and market cities of the UK together with limits of climate and topography mean that pastoral farming dominates in both regions.

7. (a) With a historic link to heavy and traditional manufacturing, such as shipbuilding on the coast and metalworking inland, ready access to raw materials accounts for the initial growth in manufacturing here.

5. (a)

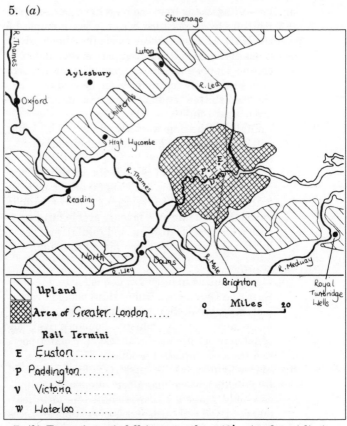

Upland

Area of Greater London.....

Rail Termini

E Euston.........
P Paddington........
V Victoria.........
W Waterloo.........

7. (b) Excessive rainfall (greater than 40in. in places) limits
   arable farming. Acid soils mean that rough grazing
   dominates. Relative under population here means
   extensive agriculture can be accommodated.

8. Highland areas and long valley floors of the Lake
   District mean that successful settlements were located
   in the valleys where trade was optimal. With steep
   topography the population are forced to engage in
   extensive pastoral farming, with valley bottoms ideal
   since sheep may then wander on the fells. Where two or
   more valleys meet, e.g. at Ambleside, a coalescence of
   positive trade factors has led to high population

densities. By contrast, East Anglia contains a network of large fields due to arable farming. Historically the local people worked the fields, with each small village serving the neighbouring farms. With limited constraints on location, the population is more evenly distributed.

PAPER II

1. (a) and (b) See overleaf
    (c) (i) Pampas: winters are cool to mild and summers are warm and humid. Rainfall in the spring and summer comes as brief heavy showers and thunderstorms, whereas more general rainfall occurs the rest of the year as cold fronts and storm systems move through. Snow may fall in winter. Prairies: winters are cold, often bringing snow, and summers are warm, sometimes with droughts.
        (ii) Rift-valley lake: when continental crust is pulled apart by convection currents in the upper mantle, the land drops into the gap and the depression is filled with water.
        Coral reef: extensive agglomerations of living coral, forming a sub-surface ridge upon which a marine ecosystem grows.

2. (a) In summer, the line of latitude that gets the maximum insolation migrates north to the Tropic of Cancer, meaning that the angle at which the sun's rays hit the UK is higher than in winter. As the sun is literally more 'overhead', shadows are shorter and daylight hours longer.
    (b) As the earth rotates, there will always be a location that has the sun directly overhead, that position merely changes. When Australia sees the sun setting, 'behind' it the UK is beginning to see sunrise.

3. (a) A wide, flat appearance with at least one river channel meandering towards the coastline. In some places there may be oxbow lakes. Channels may have natural levees on their sides and the edges of the plain may be marked by a 'step' known as a river terrace. Example: Mississippi, north of New Orleans.

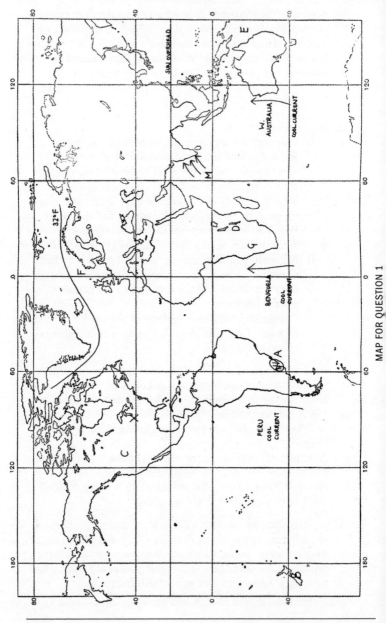

MAP FOR QUESTION 1

(b) Eroding cliffs may show caves, arches, stacks, stumps, and wave cut notches. Example: Great Ocean Road, between Melbourne and Adelaide.

(c) Fold mountains are characterized by steep jagged escarpments, deep glacial-cut valleys, frequent earthquakes, visible sedimentary layers folded in a sequence of anticlines and synclines, and enclosed glaciers with rock outcrop peaks exposed. Example: the Himalayas.

4. (a) Quito is approximately 9350ft above sea level and the adiabatic cooling effect means it is over 20°F cooler than Manaos.

(b) Vancouver is a coastal location and in winter the prevailing winds from the sea bring relative warmth, since oceans react more slowly to the seasonal swing in insolation. Winnipeg is in the middle of a large continent where the ground conducts heat away in the winter but warms up faster in the summer.

(c) Although it is winter in both places, Port Sudan lies closer to the Tropic of Cancer and the angle of incidence of the sun remains relatively high, providing relative warmth. Archangel, on the northern coast of Russia, receives insipid sunshine for shorter periods due to the low position of the sun and the curvature of the earth.

5. (a) *See overleaf*

(b) The Monsoon season followed by months of limited rainfall means that when water does arrive it must be distributed on to the land to maximize harvests. Methods used range from donkey-turned wheels with earthen pots to raise water on to fields to more complex systems of counterweights. The water spreads on to padi and is then ponded in by use of earthen banks, or 'bunds'. This system is also used in arid areas like Kashmir.

(c) Rice is produced by irrigating a padi field and planting the young plant underwater, with its shoots protruding. The padi is tended until the rice is ready for harvesting. After cutting, the ear of rice is dried in the sun and simple threshing is used. The rice is then further dried and sold.

In southern Indian states, coir is made by spinning the

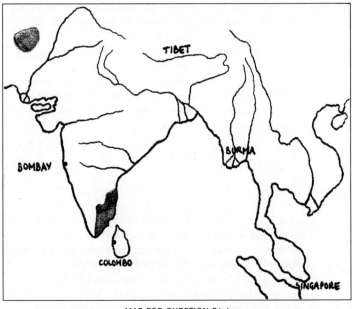

MAP FOR QUESTION 5(a)

fibres of the coconut husk, which have been removed from the shell by hand, into long ropes. This raw material is then woven into matting that is used locally, often as carpet, and even exported to the UK for items such as doormats.

6. (a) The sunny and relatively dry climate from Portugal across to Greece and the Middle East produces good yields of fruit, including grapes for winemaking.
   (b) The tropical grassland is the ideal environment for the lions, giraffe, African elephant and hippopotamus.
   (c) Sheep are reared across the country on extensive 'stations' and the wool produced is traditionally the main agricultural export.

7. (a) In Siberia, very cold winters leave the ground frozen for long periods with snow cover. In Africa, forests have a 12-month growing season with typically 2000mm of rainfall and almost constant temperatures of approximately 30°C.

(b) In Siberia there are a limited number of species, adapted to the extreme cold. Coniferous forests (Boreal forests) produce pinewood for use as paper and furniture. Tropical forests have a great variety of species reflecting the varied niche conditions.

(c) In Siberia, coniferous forests are managed as other crops, with planting, growing and harvesting done on a large scale. Trees are transported by road or river to mills, where they are either cut into congruent planks or pulped for use in the paper industry. Tropical deforestation is more destructive, since unwanted and invaluable trees are often burnt to access the expensive species that are then sawed and dragged through the forest. They are exported great distances to mills and then on to local or export manufacturers.

8. (a) Intensive farming involves the use of machinery, fertilizers and pesticides to gain larger yields, e.g. wheat farming in East Anglia. Extensive farming involves low levels of inputs and gains lower yields per field, e.g. hill sheep farming in Wales.

(b) Intensive farming: rice is grown in the Philippines using terraced fields that require large workforces to tend. Extensive farming: cattle ranches are found in the Pampas of Brazil since the semi-arid climate does not allow arable farming and the scrub grassland can be grazed over large areas.

9. (a) Tea in Ceylon requires cool mist cloud during the growing season and plenty of rain. Cotton in the USA needs a lot of water, usually acquired from extensive irrigation. Rubber in Malaysia requires a hot, wet climate that allows the plant to continue growing even when tapped.

(b) Tea is grown on extensive monoculture plantations on hillsides where rainfall is high. Leaves are picked when they are soft and this is done by hand. They are then dried, chopped, graded and packed into muslin-lined wooden crates before being exported. Cotton is also picked by hand before being washed and spun, or exported as raw cotton to be spun elsewhere. Rubber is tapped through intricate canals cut into the surface layer of the tree bark. The white sap is caught in bowls tied to the trees, which are periodically emptied and their contents cured before export.

10. In the Nile valley land by the river has been irrigated with the floodwaters. Along with warm temperatures throughout the year, the growing conditions are suitable for crops such as rice and dates. Large populations can therefore be supported. In the Amazon the volume of impenetrable vegetation has made the area unsuitable for settlements. In Siberia, the severe cold winters allow few plants to grow and only those who are able to herd local animals, such as reindeer, have colonized the area.

11. Northern Italy: the industrial heartland, with resources for traditional industries that has attracted large populations, including entrepreneurs.
South-eastern Brazil: the country's traditional focus of economic wealth, containing the cities of Rio de Janeiro and Sao Paulo.
Highlands of Peru and Ecuador: plateaus have allowed agriculture to succeed in regions where other agricultural systems have failed due to the steep land of the Andes.
Lawrence lowlands and Lake Peninsula: deep soils, laid down by the last glaciation, and an ideal climate provide agriculturally productive land.

12. (a) The removal of the fertile topsoil layer of the ground by wind or water.
    (b) Examples include the Serengeti Plain, the USA Prairie lands and Loess Plateau in China.
    (c) It is caused by the wind picking up fine fragments from the surface of the ground and removing them (deflation), or by running water washing material away (surface wash). Both processes have been exacerbated by human action, with overgrazing reducing the amount of humus in the soil and machines and animals compacting the ground so that infiltration of water is reduced.
    Prevention methods include planting wind breaks, cutting diversion channels, breaking up surface duricrusts and using organic fertilizer to maintain the soil's humus content.

HOUSEHOLD COOKERY

PAPER I

1. (a) Eggs are an important source of protein (containing all
the essential amino acids needed), a good source of all
the B vitamins (which help your body convert food into
energy, as well as ensuring normal blood formation), the
fat-soluble vitamin A (for good night vision, growth and
healthy skin), vitamin D (which help to absorb calcium
and phosphorus and for bone health), as well as some
vitamin E (an antioxidant). They contain most of the
necessary minerals, and are a good source of iodine
(which is required to make the thyroid hormone), and
phosphorus (for bone health). They provide a significant
amount of zinc (for growth and normal function of the
immune system), selenium (an antioxidant that helps
your immune system), and calcium (for bone structure,
growth and nervous function). Eggs also contain
significant amounts of iron, which is essential for red
blood cell formation. Eggs are relatively low in saturated
fat and low in calories, with only around 80 kcals per
medium egg.

(b) Breakfast – hard-boiled
Light snack – scrambled egg on toast
Cakes – Victoria sponge
Puddings – chocolate mousse
Batters – pancakes
Binding agent – burgers

2. (a) Dairy foods such as milk, cheese and yoghurt provide
calcium (for healthy teeth and bones) and other essential
nutrients, including protein, phosphorous, vitamins A, D
and B12, riboflavin, niacin and potassium.
Foods in the meat group provide protein (for strong
muscles and repairing body tissue), iron (for red blood
cell formation), B vitamins (for energy), vitamin E, zinc
and magnesium. As well as meat itself, food in this group
includes fish, dry beans, tofu, eggs, nuts and seeds.
Fruits and vegetables provide vitamins A (for night vision
and healthy skin and eyes) and C (for healing and

fighting infection), potassium (to regulate blood pressure), fibre (for regular digestion) and other nutrients.

Grain group foods provide complex carbohydrates (for energy) and fibre. Foods in this group include breads, cereals, rice, pasta, etc.

Other minor groups include fats and sugars.

(b) Milk – dairy group
Butter – fat group
Carrots – fruit and vegetables group
Oatmeal – grain group
Jam – sugar group

3. (a) Remove and throw away badly discoloured and wilted outside leaves (The outer leaves contain most of the vitamins and mineral salts). Cut the cabbage into quarters to ensure even cooking, removing the stalk if very thick, and wash well in salted water. Rinse in fresh water and drain. Shred, cutting from the outside to the stalk. Add to boiling, salted water or stock, allowing about ¼ pint for each 2lb of cabbage. Cover the pan and cook for 10–15 minutes, or until the cabbage is tender, shaking the pan occasionally to prevent burning. Drain well.

(b) Beat 2 eggs, add 1 pint of milk and a pinch of salt. Strain into a greased pie-dish and stir in 1oz of sugar. Grate nutmeg or orange or lemon rind over the custard or add orange or lemon essence. Bake for 1 hour at gas mark 1 or for 40 minutes at gas mark 2.

(c) Melt 1oz of butter or margarine in a saucepan. Add 1oz of flour and, stirring continuously, cook for a few minutes without browning. Gradually add ½ to ¾ pint of liquid such as milk, milk and water, or stock, stirring carefully. Boil for 5–10 minutes to cook the flour. Add any flavouring required. The sauce should be smooth and thick enough to coat the back of a wooden spoon.

4. (i) A lack of seasoning; failure to trim the meat of fat before cooking; and failure to seal/brown the meat before stewing

(ii) Adding insufficient cornflour to 'set' the mould; not mixing it in properly; or not boiling the sauce to cook the cornflour

(iii) Overworking; not sifting the flour; insufficient raising agent; insufficient liquid; the oven being too cool; baking for too long; or the baking position being too low

5. (a) Good ingredients: it should be made from quality, dry flour; lard has the most 'shortening power' (which makes the pastry rich and crisp), though butter has the best flavour; salt must be used to bring out the full flavour of the flour; water must be very cold and freshly drawn. All the ingredients must be kept cool, and a cold knife or cool hands used to mix the ingredients. Work as quickly and lightly as possible, and do not overwork the dough. Do not use too much water, and mix in evenly. When rolling out the pastry, do not flour the work surface too liberally. Bake in a preheated oven at a high temperature.

(b) Baking the pastry ingredients at a high temperature quickly 'sets' the dough and prevents it from becoming tough or shrinking. It also ensures that the fat doesn't ooze out, and gives a crisp, firm result.

6. When creaming together the fat and sugar, the ingredients should be at room temperature and the mixture pale and fluffy. Eggs should be beaten in well, one at a time, then the flour folded in, half at a time, with a metal spoon. A little milk should be added. The container for steaming must be half-filled with water and heated so that it is boiling by the time the pudding is made. The basin needs to be well greased and filled no more than two-thirds full with the mixture. The basin should be covered with buttered greaseproof paper or foil, with a pleat in the middle to allow the pudding to rise. It should be tightly secured with string to prevent steam or water entering, and a string handle should be fashioned for easy lifting in and out of the water. The lid of the saucepan or steamer must fit tightly to reduce loss of steam. The water in the steamer must boil rapidly throughout the cooking process, and be topped up regularly with boiling water to avoid it boiling dry.

7. (i) Suet: remove all the skin and chop finely, sprinkling some of the flour over whilst chopping. Add it to sifted flour, baking powder and salt. Mix with cold water to form a soft dough.

   (ii) Butter: cut the chilled fat into walnut-sized pieces. Add to a bowl containing sifted flour and salt. Stir using a palette knife, with enough lemon juice or cold water to form a stiff dough.

  (iii) Butter or margarine: melt gently in a saucepan, adding the flour and stirring continuously until free of lumps.

  (iv) Butter or margarine: melt in a saucepan then add the sugar, syrup, treacle or beaten eggs. Stir over a low heat until the sugar is dissolved and allow to cool before adding to the other ingredients.

   (v) Butter or margarine: allow the fat to reach room temperature and beat thoroughly with the sugar using a wooden spoon until pale and fluffy.

PAPER II

1. (a) Milk is a major source of protein (for growth and repair of the body), calcium (for strong bones and teeth), B vitamins (which help to release energy into the body) and minerals such as zinc and magnesium (for immunity and energy). Vitamins A (for healthy skin, growth and vision) and D are found in whole milk and its products.

  (b) By keeping the milk cool in the fridge or larder or placing the bottle in a bowl of cold water and covering with a damp cloth.

2. (a) Vegetables are an important source of mineral salts and vitamins, green vegetables being particularly valuable for vitamin C. To prevent vitamin loss, choose freshly cut, crisp vegetables and serve raw when possible, as most of the mineral salts and vitamins B and C are water soluble. Over-boiling leads to vitamin loss. Retain liquid for making sauces, soups or gravy. Serve vegetables immediately after cooking.

  (b) Cooking food quickly to retain flavour, colour, texture and nutrients.

3. (a) To make batter: sift 4oz of flour and a pinch of salt into a bowl. Make a well in the centre, add 1 egg and beat well using a wooden spoon. Add ½ pint of milk gradually, drawing in the flour to make a smooth batter.

Beat well and leave to stand in a cool place for 1 hour before using.

To make pancakes: heat a little fat in a frying pan until hot, running it around the base and sides of the pan and pouring off any excess. Pour in enough batter to coat the base of the pan thinly. Cook over a medium flame until golden brown, shake the pan to prevent sticking, then turn or toss and cook the other side until golden.

To make a Yorkshire pudding: melt 1oz of lard or dripping in a meat tin and, when it is smoking hot, pour in the batter and bake in the oven for 35–40 minutes at gas mark 7.

(b) Thorough beating mixes in plenty of air, although thick batters containing baking powder should be beaten only enough to make a smooth mixture. Allow batter to stand to give the starch grains in the flour time to swell and produce a lighter consistency. Beat again 5 minutes before using to prevent separation.

4. Simmer: to cook in liquid just below boiling point (at about 185°F), e.g. poached egg.

Sauté: a quick-cooking process in which foods are browned in a little fat in a pan on the hotplate, e.g. onions.

Clarify (fat): to remove sediment or impurities from butter or dripping so that they can be used for frying at high temperatures, e.g. some sponge mixes.

Steaming: to cook food in the steam from boiling water, e.g. Christmas pudding.

Au gratin: a term applied to dishes covered with breadcrumbs or grated cheese and browned in the oven or underneath the grill, e.g. Dauphinoise potatoes.

Batter: a smooth mixture of flour, egg, milk and water (and sometimes yeast), used to coat foods to be fried, baked as a pudding, or fried as a pancake, e.g. Yorkshire pudding.

Purée: cooked food rubbed through a sieve or reduced to a pulp, e.g. babyfood or potatoes.

5. (a) 1oz fat and 1oz flour to 1 pint of liquid.

(b) Cheese sauce: add 2–4oz of grated cheese, for Cauliflower au Gratin. Onion sauce: add 2 large peeled and chopped onions, boiled in salted water until soft, for serving with roast lamb. Parsley sauce: add 1 heaped tablespoon of finely chopped parsley, to pour over grilled fish.

(c) The roux should not be allowed to colour, so cook fat and flour on a low temperature. To avoid lumps, the liquid should be added slowly and stirred carefully. To ensure the flour is cooked and the sauce thickened it should be cooked for at least 5 minutes.

6. (a) To seal the flavour
   (b) To aerate the flour and ensure a light result, as well as getting rid of any lumps
   (c) To enable the cheese to melt evenly and quickly
   (d) To ensure the food is sealed properly before cooking through
   (e) To speed up the first rising process

7. Protein foods are vital for growth, tissue repair, immune function, the manufacture of essential hormones and enzymes, the preservation of lean muscle mass, and for the production of energy when carbohydrate is not available. They are also broken down by digestion into essential amino acids.
   (i) Pulses, nuts and grains
   (ii) Meat, shellfish and dairy products
   (iii) Eggs, fish and poultry

MUSIC

SECTION A

1. (ii), (x), (ix), (vi), (v), (viii), (iv), (iii), (i), (vii)

2. Music: for vocalists – ayres, canzonets and madrigals; for instrumentalists – fantasties, variation forms e.g. variations, rounds and grounds, and dances, including pavan, galliard, alman and jig
   Instruments: keyboard instruments such as the virginal, harpsichord, spinet, and occasionally the organ; plucked string instruments including lute, cittern and Pandora; bowed string instruments including viols; recorders.

3. It used expanded musical forms more free of the constraints of the classical period, had extra-musical references, and used music to reflect emotional themes. Specifically:

   • Berlioz made use of grand scale orchestration typical of the Romantic period e.g. in the *Te Deum* and *Requiem*; he used texts and non-musical sources to influence his music, particularly in *Symphonie fantastique*, which came with considerable programme text; he used recurring themes, or 'idées fixes', e.g. in *Harold in Italy*.

   • Schumann used literary ideas to influence his music, e.g. in the *Papillons*, influenced by Jean Paul's *Flegeljahre*; he used highly lyrical melodic lines, e.g. in the *Fantasiestücke* and *Kinderszenen*; he utilized new forms of music in the short, expressive 'salon' style piano pieces he composed.

   • Dvorak worked in the romantic symphonic poem form; like many romantic composers he employed themes of nationalism in his music, making use of rhythms and themes from folk music in his works, for example in his *Slavonic Dances*; he used new romantic forms such as the symphonic poem (e.g. *The Water Goblin* and *The Noon Witch*); he utilized romantic harmonies and lyrical melodies, for example in his opera *Rusalka*.

4. Purcell was an early proponent of English opera, most famously *Dido and Aeneas*.

He was master organist at the Chapel Royal and Westminster Abbey, in which capacity he composed 65 anthems and composed music for 40 plays. He also composed music for royal celebrations such as the Birthday Odes.

He brought Italian and French influences (for example the light orchestral styling and court styling of Lully) to his music, particularly his sonatas, while retaining an English sound.

He composed over 500 works, which have influenced many great English composers, including Benjamin Britten, who used a Purcell theme in his *Young Person's Guide to the Orchestra*.

5. Bach and Handel utilized counterpoint, i.e. two or more lines of melodically interesting material (as opposed to just harmony) that sound simultaneously.

    Bach's use of polyphony is particularly pronounced in his keyboard collections, such as his inventions, preludes and fugues, partitas and the English and French Suites. The opening movement of the *St Matthew Passion* is a prime example, making use of 8 weaving choral parts.

    Handel made use of polyphony in his keyboard writing, for example in his keyboard suites, and he wrote a number of polyphonic stand-alone fugues for keyboard, for example *The Messiah*, 'And with his stripes' and 'He trusted in God'.

6. An extended sacred or ethical work or text, which is often biblical or non-liturgical. Examples include: Bach's masses (liturgica), passions and Easter and Ascension Oratorios; Schütz's *Resurrection* and passions; Handel's *Saul*, *Samson* and *Israel in Egypt*.

    Oratios differ from opera in that they are non-dramatic for lack of costume, acting and staging and so are not for the theatre, though the music itself may be dramatic; they are religious in feeling and content unlike operas; and some employ hymns, e.g. chorales in Bach, and plainsong in Mozart's *Requiem*.

7. Composers of the symphony following the death of C.P.E. Bach include: J.C. Bach, Hofman, Dittersdorf, Vauhal, Michael Haydn, Stamitz. Joseph Haydn, Mozart, Beethoven, and Schubert.

Sonatas have changed form from their initial appearance in the baroque era, when the term was used to describe a variety of works, normally fugues and toccatas, played either by solo or by a group of instruments. In the classical era (particularly under Joseph Haydn, Mozart and Beethoven), 'sonata form' came to mean a piece of music typically in three or four movements, and increasingly throughout the period it was performed by a solo instrument accompanied by a piano or ensemble, rather than the chamber sonatas of the baroque period.

The symphony is normally orchestral. Early examples typically had three movements – which followed a quick-slow-quick structure, with at least the first movement in binary form. In the classical period, most notably under Joseph Haydn, the four-movement symphony structure was standardized. Mozart expanded its scale, with complex orchestral textures and a more emotional expression, e.g. symphonies 38–41. The Romantic period saw Beethoven expanding movements further (e.g. symphony no. 3 *Eroica*), adding soloists in his symphony no. 9 and a chorus to express universal kinship. At the beginning of the twentieth century, Mahler wrote long, extended symphonies, using much more romantic, textured harmonies, and leitmotifs. In the twentieth century Sibelius composed a one-movement symphony (no. 7), and composers such as Messiaen and Philip Glass diversified the form further still.

SECTION B (i)

1. Similarities are that they are all polyphonic, each voice/line copies each other (at the unison or octave) or there is imitation (at a different pitch).

   They differ in that a round merely copies: e.g. 'Sumer is icumin in' occurs over a two-part ostinaro, making up a rondellus, whereas canonic imitation may be at a different pitch. Unlike the round or fugue, canonic imitation may be inverted, retrograde, augmented or diminished in note lengths, or combinations of these. The fugue contains imitation and non-imitative material, and sometimes includes a canon. Unlike a round or canon, the fugue must start with an exposition.

2. Examples include: Renaissance sacred vocal music (e.g. the motet in *In Ecclesiis* by Giovanni Gabrieli and Byrd's masses for 3, 4 and 5 voices), the canzona, which was first applied to vocal music, then additionally to instrumental music, Ricercave, which is represented by ensembles in motet style in Cavazzoni on the organ (1543), canons and fugues, and much baroque music, for example preludes, fantasies, toccatas and inventions.

3. A triple metre movement, often before the finale of a symphony or sonata in da capo form (ABA). Originally, the trio was for three instruments, but this restriction could not apply in solo sonatas, and was lifted in symphonies. Examples include Haydn's Symphony 97 in C major (third mvt), Mozart's 39th (3rd mvt) and Beethoven's Septet (op. 20).

4. Bach and his contemporaries used more counterpoint whereas Beethoven et al. made more use of melody accompanied by harmony; their concertos were not as extended as Beethoven's (who regularly used cadenzas for example); Bach and his contemporaries commonly used concerto grosso, whereas Beethoven's and later composers' work are solo concertos; Bach et al.'s concertos utilized smaller orchestras, e.g. only flute, violin and harpsichord in the slow movement of the Brandenburg Concerto no. 5 in D, whereas in Beethoven's the continuo had gone, the orchestra filled out the chords, and woodwind and brass instruments came in pairs; Beethoven and later composers used new instruments, some of which replaced those of Bach and his comtemporaries, e.g. his keyboard was the piano, the viols of Bach's Brandenburg no. 6 in B flat had become obsolete, and the clarinet was another addition.

5. The aria da capo form is an accompanied song of the seventeenth and eighteenth centuries where the original material returns after a contrasting middle section, sometimes summarized as ABA, e.g. 'He was despised' from Handel's *Messiah*.

SECTION B (ii)

1. ♦ The organ – wind at pressure is controlled by a mixture of keys and stops, before reaching the pipes; there are usually two 'manuals' or keyboards for the hands, and pedals for the feet; stops control different timbres and pitches (octaves and harmonics).

   ♦ Virginal – this is plucked with a plectrum or quill and has strings parallel to the keyboard.

   ♦ Spiner – as above but with strings at the diagonal.

   ♦ Harpsichord – has strings running away from the player, with a few controls for different timbres and pitches often having two manuals and three choirs (sets of strings); its comparably loud volume allowed it to be used in orchestral pieces.

   ♦ Clavichord – a tangent strikes the string; like the piano, it is possible to hit the string with varying degrees of force; unlike the piano it doe this very quietly, and it can produce a vibrato.

2. Examples include *The Phantasiestücke*, *Kinderszenen and Papillons*. They differ from the works of Handel in that they are Romantic in nature, with the pieces and their titles evocative of literary and other extra-musical matters; they use a larger pianistic spread and occasionally demand greater virtuosity than Handel's work; Handel's piano music is baroque, and consequently more contrapuntal than Schumann's; while Handel's movements are often based on various dances, they do not have illustrative titles.

3. Some of the compositions Bach wrote for the organ include:

   ♦ Chorale fugue – e.g. *Wir Glauben all' an Einen Gott*, Schopfer BWV680

   ♦ Chorale prelude – e.g. In dir ist Freude BWV 608 from the *Orgelbüchlein*

   ♦ Chorale fantasia – e.g. *Komm, Heiliger Geist* BWV 651

   ♦ Preludes and fugues – e.g. In D major BWV 532, F minor BWV 534, in E major 'St Anne' BWV 552, and numerous others

- ◆ Fantasias – e.g. in C minor BWV 562, and in G major BWV 572
- ◆ Trio sonatas – BWV 525-530
- ◆ Passacaglia and fugue – in C minor BWV 582

4. Beethoven's scherzo is often the third movement of four within a sonata, but Chopin's four scherzos each stand alone; Beethoven's classical scherzos were more amenable to development compared to Chopin's short, symmetrical phrases; Chopin used influences from Polish folk music and Italian operatic melody; Beethoven's harmonies are more chordal than Chopin's chromatization; the structure of Beethoven's scherzos is akin to a fast minuet, whereas Chopin's is more unpredictable in form.

5. The sound was actuated on the harpsichord by a quill plectrum, and on the piano by a hammer of wood clothed by a softer cushion, e.g. felt, giving a more mellow timbre; changes of volume on the harpsichord depend on the registers played, whereas the on the piano the use of more physical force through the arms allows a far more powerful sound; the piano has a sustaining pedal, which can add colour, volume and fluidity.

   New effects were employed by using arpeggios right across the keyboard, thanks to the sustaining pedal; making greater use of volume changes, and sforzandi; expecting greater virtuosity from the pianists; and using much larger chords.

SECTION B (iii)

1. The pianoforte was used to add dramatic colour, for example in Schubert's *Erlkönig* the fast triplet octaves in the right hand of the piano depict a galloping horse, and create a sense of urgency; when death speaks the piano changes to a fiendishly fast waltz rhythm. It also provided rich harmonies, for example Schubert uses tremulo and dimished chords in *Die Stadt*, which also create a sense of dread. The pianoforte offered rhythmic accompaniment, and the option to play with rhythms, for examples in Vaughan Williams' *Songs of Travel*, the accompaniment of 'In Dreams' is pushed off beat, adding to the sense of melancholy. Occasionally it took up the tune, for example in 'Nun hast du mir' by

Schumann, the piano has some crushing chords, but ends quoting the first song in the cycle, but pianissimo, and effectively distant.

2. 'Song cycle' refers to a group of songs, conceived as an entity, usually having a common thread of meaning or narrative. A good example is *Die schöne Müllerin*, a setting of twenty poems by Wilhelm Müller.

3. Most usual types were recitatives and arias. These could be free-standing, paired, or embedded in extended works such as opera, oratorios or cantatas. Recitatives were fast-flowing as speech and could feature dialogue or thought. Aria were sung, although some were strophic. Most seventeenth-century arias were in the form of ABB1 (1 = short) or the da capo aria, ABA or ABA1.

4. ◆ Wolf – Austrian composer of 245 published songs, and 103 unpublished or posthumously published. His most well-known pieces are the *Spanisches Liederbuch*, and two volumes of *Italienisches Liederbuch*. He is particularly noted for using his music to reflect the text faithfully. His song cycles encompass a wide range of mood, dark and light. He made expressive use of the piano accompaniment to assist mood and structure.

   ◆ Schumann – composed over 300 songs (including the cycles *Frauenliebe und Leben*, and *Dichterliebe*), roughly 70 part songs, 30 duets and trios. His works are deeply Romantic in their use of extra-musical reference and programmatic content, for example *Frauenliebe und Leben* depicts the flowering of a woman's love, marriage, giving birth and her husband's death. He favoured the piano accompaniment, often leaving it playing alone at the conclusion of a song.

   ◆ Mendelssohn – German Romantic composer who wrote 6 concert arias, 70 songs and 12 duets. Although he was a Romantic composer, he leant towards classical clarity. His songs were particularly finely crafted, and used especially sweet cantabile lines that were popular with singers.

   ◆ Warlock – this Anglo-Welsh composer wrote many songs, and is celebrated especially for *The Curlew*, which used a string quartet, flute and cor anglais to accompany a tenor voice. His music is influenced by Delius and Bartok, and utilizes modal lines, and distinctive chord structures as well as sliding parallel chromaticisms. He often used medieval poems as the text for his songs.

◆ Stanford – an Irish composer, well known in his day for his choral works. He figured prominently in the rebirth of British composition and his influences included Brahms and Schumann (he studied in Germany), with his melodies often informed by Irish folksong. His choral works include a Requiem, motets and anthems. He also wrote some sensitive part songs, including the popular 'The Blue Bird'.

Or

4. ◆ Schubert – he composed over 600 songs, including the famous cycles *Die Schöne Müllerin*, *Winterreise*, and *Schwanengesang*. It was in the genre of the Lied that he made his greatest contribution to the art of the song, bringing greater dramatic content, using increasingly innovative harmonies, modulations and dissonances and making greater pictorial use of the piano accompaniment. Schubert also wrote religious works such as psalms and masses, and other secular writings for voice include an oratorio, *Lazarus*, as well as operas and music for theatre.

◆ Dowland – this English composer wrote 84 airs for voice and lute, raising the level of English song. His first book of airs had four editions in his lifetime and his music was promoted in eight European cities. He used discordant harmonies to great effect, e.g. in 'In darknesse let me dwell'. In some respects he could be called the first 'modern' songwriter, for his ability to make his music reflect the emotional content of the text of the songs.

◆ Parry – he was largely responsible for the renaissance of English music, evolving a 'diatonic' style that was to greatly influence composers that followed him. His music was deeply nationalistic, with one of his unison songs, 'Jerusalem', still being used as an anthem for the English nation. Influenced by Bach, his part songs are, unusually, contrapuntal. Of his choral works, the *Songs of Farewell* are much loved.

◆ Brahms – this German Romantic composer composed 200 Lieder. He wrote two song cycles, both with symphonic style accompaniment: *Romanzen* and *Magelone*, and *Vier ernste Gesänge*. Brahms' songs idealize the folk music style, and he even composed a set of pseudo-gypsy songs, entitled *Zigeunerlieder*.

SECTION B (iv)

1. (*a*) The trumpet, horn, trombone and orchestral tuba.
   (*b*) Brass instruments' sound is produced by air passing through the lips, which are stretched across the mouthpiece. This is known as lip vibrating. Notes of different pitch are made by altering the tension of the lips. Notes in between those of the harmonica series are obtained through the use of three valves under the pistons or levers, except for the trombone, which has its telescopic slide. Because the notes of the harmonic series are not in tune with most temperaments in use, adjustments are made with the lips. Trumpets and horns have used crooks to transpose to easier keys.

2. (*a*) Violin – tune by upwards 5ths, starting an octave below G, i.e. G, D, A, E.
   Viola – tune in upwards 5ths, starting an octave below middle C, so C, D, G, A.
   Cello – tune an octave below the violin.
   Double bass – tune in 4ths starting on E, nearly 3 octaves below middle C, so E, A, D, G.
   (*b*) 'Pizzicato' means to play the strings by plucking them with the fingers; 'arco' means to play the strings with the bow; 'con sordino' means to attach a mute to the bridge to veil the tone; 'double-stopping' means playing two notes simultaneously on different strings.

3. The functions of the harpsichord player were to play continuo, to direct the performance and to provide harmonies. The harpsichord player is not necessary in modern orchestral music because composers write more harmonies in the other orchestral instruments, violinists lead the performance, and the double bass player provides continuo effect. As directing became more demanding, conductors also became necessary.

4. The purpose of the continuo was to provide harmonies, often a bass line and improvised harmonies, which might be shared with another instrument; to extemporize harmony, provide movement and help create atmosphere, e.g. the earthquake in *St Matthew Passion*; and to provide suitable timbre, whether harpsichord, lute or organ.

5. ◆ Bass clarinet – Liszt, Mayerbeer, Wagner, Tchaikovsky

   ◆ Orchestral tuba – Wagner, Elgar, Strauss

   ◆ Saxophone – Mayerbeer, Massenet, Bizet

   ◆ Side drum – Strauss, Wagner, Liszt

   ◆ Gong – Tchaikovsky (used by Spontini in 1807)

   ◆ Bells – Holst

   ◆ Xylophone – Saint-Saëns, Mahler

SECTION B (v)

1. Originally composers did not specify which instruments should play, whereas Haydn set the precedent for deliberately choosing instruments for each part. Consorts of viols or recorders, or mixed consorts, were replaced by string quartets and solo performers. The old domestic fantasies and dances were replaced by string quartets and solo sonatas.

2. The string quartet. Haydn wrote between 65 and 80 string quartets; some are disputed, others are arrangements. He standardized the four-movement form, and introduced the scherzo in the opus 33 set nos. 2 and 3, 'The Joke' and 'The Bird'. Haydn was influenced by the literary movement of *Sturm und Drang* (e.g. his *Farewell* Symphony), and later, by Mozart's lyricism.

   Mozart himself composed twenty-seven string quartets, six of which were dedicated to Haydn. He developed the form, making increasing use of key changes, and full dramatic dialogue between the instruments. The string quartet was further developed under Beethoven, who composed seventeen. He made the movements longer; used increasingly daring harmony and made exciting use of counterpoint between the instruments; went further than

Mozart in use of modulations to distant keys; and used an increasingly Romantic sense of drama.

3. The sopranino, descant, treble, tenor and bass, great bass and double bass.

4. Early string consort compositions for viol and voice could be much alike, and perhaps the instrumentation depended on availability of players.

    Composers include Orlando Gibbon, whose madrigals were published as 'apt', e.g. The Cries of London; Wilbye, whose Second Book of Madrigals was 'apt' for voices and viols; and Giuseppe Gerbino whose Third Book of Madrigals was 'apt' for both.

    The viol family were bowed instruments, usually with six strings. They were held vertically on the lap or between the legs (da gamba), depending on their size. Their tuning intervals were irregular, but in the same sequence (e.g. the treble was D, G, C^1; the tenor started up from G; the bass from D, an octave below the treble). The viols became popular in the sixteenth century and survived well into the eighteenth century in England, through the popularity of Purcell's Fantasias. C.P.E. Bach also continued to use them.

5. The essential differences are: in Corelli's works the harmony was often improvised from the bass line, whereas in Haydn's piano trios the whole piano part was written out by the composer; although the pianoforte of Haydn's time was more like a harpsichord than a modern piano, it had a more generous and colourful tone than that of Corelli's time, allowing for more expressive performances; and that due to the greater degree of control in the pianoforte of Haydn's time, it could be used as an equal part with lines acting as answering phrases in a conversation with the other instruments, unlike the comparatively simple continuo part of Corelli's period.

SECTION B (vi)

1. Forms included:

   - Mass – Byrd wrote these for three, four and five voices. They consisted of several movements: Kyrie, Gloria, Credo, Sonatas, Benedictus, Agnus Dei and sometimes Ite missa est. The text was from the 'ordinary', i.e. the fixed order of the mass vote. Its texture was usually polyphonic.

   - Motet – including Tallis' 40-part *Spem im alium*, and Giovanni Gabrieli's *In Ecclesiis*. The motet was usually a single movement of scored music. Any religious text might be used if appropriate for the occasion, usually in Latin. Like the mass, the motet was usually polyphonic.

   - Anthem – this was similar to the motet, except that it was prescribed to be in English; in a simpler texture than the polyphonic motet; was sometimes strophic and is called English verse anthem, e.g. Byrd's Easter Anthem, 'Christ rising again'.

   - Psalms – e.g. Schutz's *Psalmen Davids*. The text for psalms was taken from the Bible, and had to be appropriate for the occasion.

   - Madrigal – e.g. Morley's 'Now is the month of Maying'. The madrigal was often a single movement; sometimes in sections, sometimes strophic. The text was poetic, ranging from the trivial to the philosophical.

2. The chorale was a hymn sung by the congregation. It would be recognized by the layperson when it was incorporated into new compositions, where it might be a separate movement or part of the texture. Works for organ include: chorale preludes, normally improvised but the best were written down e.g. In dulci jubilo, BWV 608 from das Orgelbüchlein by Bach; chorale fuges, e.g. *Wir glauben all an einen Gott Schöpfer*, BVW 680; chorale fantasia, e.g. *Komm, heiliger Geist*, BWV 651; and chorale variations, e.g. *Vonn Himmel hoch*, BWV 769.

3. Mendelssohn's contribution included his many compositions for vocal groups, including: the oratories *St Paul* and *Elijah*; around thirty psalms; sacred and secular cantatas, for

example *Die erste Walpurgisnacht*; various motets and
anthems; sixty choral songs. An eighteenth-century
composer and musician, he conducted a revival performance
of Bach's *St Matthew Passion*. He was highly influenced by
Bach's fugues, Handel's rhythms and Mozart's sense of
drama, and he used these qualities to bring polyphonic
scoring to Romantic choral music.

4. The Chapel Royal's records go back to 1135. It was a body of
clergy and musicians, and boys in training. In the sixteenth
century, their staff numbered over a hundred. Under the
reign of Elizabeth I, Tallis, Byrd, and Gibbons served in the
Chapel Royal. After a pause for the Commonwealth
(1649–1660) came Pelham Humfrey and Purcell. More
latterly, Elgar and Bliss were Masters at the Chapel Royal.
Before the nineteenth-century schools of music, talented
youths received their training at cathedral schools and sang
in the cathedral choir. In their most glorious period,
England had composers such as Tavener and Tallis at
Waltham Abbey, Gibbons at Westminster and Morley at
St Paul's; in the eighteenth century came Blow and Boyce.
More latterly, cathedral choirs were rejuvenated by
S.S. Wesley and Stanford. Both Chapel Royal and the
cathedrals played an essential role in creating a tradition of
fine choirs and outstanding choral composition.

5. A madrigal is a short piece, usually in one movement,
sometimes in sections, sometimes strophic, consisting of a
poem set to music (therefore usually secular) and usually for
at least three voices, often four to six. It may be set for fewer
voices with accompaniment, e.g. Monteverdi's 7th Book of
Madrigals (duets for high voices), and various solo madrigals
by Caccini and d'India. Venice was the first major centre of
madrigal compositions, e.g. Arcadelt, Willaert, and Rore.
After Palestrina and Lassus, Monteverdi composed nine
books of them. Yonge's collection of translated Italian
madrigals, *Musica Transalpina* (1588), helped to enthuse
the English. Morley collected works from twenty-one
madrigal composers for 'The Triumphs of Oriana'. More
lighter-hearted examples include John Farmer's 'Fair
Phyllis' and John Bennett's 'O sleep, fond fancie'.

ACKNOWLEDGEMENTS

Grateful thanks to Dr Martin Stephen for writing the excellent Foreword; and to Veronica Persey at AQA for providing access to the question papers.

Gratitude is also due to the following contributors, who supplied the guideline answers to the questions. In alphabetical order:

Lindsay Davies, Hannah Knowles, Wendy Marx, Chris Rowland, Brenda Symons, Will Williams, and Lucy Wood.